The Classroom

THE CLASSROOM

ENCOUNTER AND ENGAGEMENT

Alan A. Block

THE CLASSROOM
Copyright © Alan A. Block, 2014.

Softcover reprint of the hardcover 1st edition 2014 978-1-137-44922-1

All rights reserved.

The following Bob Dylan lyrics reproduced with permission: "Mississippi" © 1997 by Special Rider Music, "Not Dark Yet" © 1997 by Special Rider Music, "Sign On The Window" © 1970 by Big Sky Music; renewed 1998 by Big Sky Music. Lyrics from "One of Us" by Joan Osborne, reproduced courtesy of Eric Bazilian. Lyrics from "Julian of Norwich" by Sydney Carter, reproduced by permission of Stainer & Bell Ltd, London, England www.stainer.co.uk. Parts of chapter 3 were originally published as "Asking Questions" in *ENCOUNTER*, 2010 Spring, Volume 23:1. Parts of the book were originally published as "The Book that Changed My Life or, What I Didn't Read on My Summer's Vacation" in *JCT: An Interdisciplinary Journal of Curriculum Studies*, 1999, Volume 15:4.

First published in 2014 by PALGRAVE MACMILLAN® in the United States— a division of St. Martin's Press LLC, 175 Fifth Avenue, New York, NY 10010.

Where this book is distributed in the UK, Europe and the rest of the world, this is by Palgrave Macmillan, a division of Macmillan Publishers Limited, registered in England, company number 785998, of Houndmills, Basingstoke, Hampshire RG21 6XS.

Palgrave Macmillan is the global academic imprint of the above companies and has companies and representatives throughout the world.

Palgrave® and Macmillan® are registered trademarks in the United States, the United Kingdom, Europe and other countries.

ISBN 978-1-349-49670-9   ISBN 978-1-137-44923-8 (eBook)
DOI 10.1057/9781137449238

Library of Congress Cataloging-in-Publication Data

Block, Alan A., 1947–
  The classroom : encounter and engagement / Alan A. Block.
      pages cm.
  Includes bibliographical references and index.

  1. Classroom environment.   2. Education—Environmental aspects.
I. Title.
LB3013.B543 2014
371.102'4—dc23   2014015219

A catalogue record of the book is available from the British Library.

Design by SPi Global.

First edition: October 2014

10 9 8 7 6 5 4 3 2 1

To Dan, whose conversation led me to and through this writing; to the many students with whom I have had the privilege to learn; and to Emma and Anna Rose, whose love has sustained me.

Contents

1 On the Beginnings of Ends and the
   Ends of Beginnings   1
2 Why Read the Book?   21
3 On the Asking of Questions   51
4 Saint Joan in the Classroom   67
5 The Last Lesson   87
6 Cabins, Pequods, and Classrooms   129

Afterword(s)?   171
William F. Pinar

Bibliography   181

Index   185

CHAPTER 1

ON THE BEGINNINGS OF ENDS AND THE ENDS OF BEGINNINGS

A First Step: (On the Impossibility of this Preface to a Series of Prefaces)

I HAD SET AS MY SABBATICAL PROJECT TO WRITE A SERIES OF PREFACES. I had originally planned to write prefaces for books I would never have the opportunity or the time to write. In this endeavor, I thought, I might design where I was going and see, perhaps, where I had been. These planned and forever-to-be-unwritten books represented life-long concerns that had been left behind on the road to somewhere else. Nevertheless, I believed that these prefaces would serve as appropriate markers where once I had considered pausing before traveling on to seek the Wizard in the Emerald City. After all, I considered, what else were prefaces but summaries of anticipated adventures? What else would a preface be but a road map for an anticipated undertaking?

But from the outset I was beset by problems and contradictions. I understood that I was attempting to introduce where I was going as if I had been already there; I realized that my task compelled me to describe the path on which I would venture before I had taken more than a single step. I was going to construct a preface for material I had not yet learned. My prefaces were travel plans without the anticipation of travel; I was arranging lists no bucket would ever hold. I felt confounded by the contradictions.

Fortunately, I had learned in my previous studies that I was not obligated to solve these contradictions so much as to continue to struggle with them; I need not resolve the contradictions so much as explain why these seeming contradictions were not illogicalities at all! I was learning that I couldn't write a preface for a book I had not written because, as I attempted to do so, I came to understand that the function of the preface was to describe not where I was going but, rather, where I had been. What I had originally thought of as a preface turned out to be, in fact, more like an afterword. But I hadn't yet been anywhere! Even this preface to a series of prefaces might be considered a starting point, but where it might lead remained unknown. And I understood that it was this uncertainty that provided all the excitement of the journey. I *shouldn't* know exactly where I was going if I was going to learn anything along the way: I couldn't write a preface until the end of the journey. But I had taken no journey; I couldn't write a preface.

In education it is taught that the statement of aim—the stated objective—is essential to the classroom; without this aim the classroom is deemed without direction, rudderless, without purpose. The objective—a preface in a classroom setting?—is a statement written by the teacher (or a textbook author) defining exactly what the student will learn during this particular class period, even as I considered a preface to be the destination toward which a reader might be directed. During the twentieth and twenty-first centuries these educational objectives have taken on an importance of biblical dimensions: without them, it is claimed, there is no lesson and can be no learning. But like my prefaces, these objectives for the student were accounts not of the journey but of the destination, and the existence of such objectives precluded adventure *and* learning. John Dewey (1910/1991, 208) remarks, "If the statement of the aim is taken too seriously by the instructor, as meaning more than a signal to attention, its probable result is forestalling the pupil's own reaction, relieving him of the responsibility of developing a problem and thus arresting his mental initiative." An objective defines what is to be learned, and all of the remainder of activity and learning is irrelevant. The presence of objectives suggests that there should be no adventure in education. In fact, I thought, objectives obstruct the educational journey rather than facilitate it: they keep asleep the curiosity so essential to learning. No wonder students suffer such boredom in the classroom!

My anticipated prefaces would be like those objectives: they would define the ending without having to engage in any beginning. My prefaces would make any journey irrelevant because the destination was already present at the outset: in these prefaces my gaze would be fixed on some end without any thought of means. And I came to understand that it wasn't prefaces I could write because, really, I didn't know where I was going. Nor was it objectives I wanted to construct. Rather, it was in huckleberrying I wished to engage with the classroom—in which I have spent most of my life—as my beginning, my means, and my destination. My anticipated prefaces became transformed into pedagogical journeys in the classroom where existed my uncertain past, my pleasantly confused present, and the voyages I would now undertake. What I would know at the end was in the present unknown to me. Who I would be at the end was not who was now writing. I had some starting points but I did not know where they might lead. I considered this lack of objective the interesting point. How could I have ever thought of writing a preface for what I had not yet written?

But I did want to consider some things in which I had taken some interest during my life in the light of my present life both in and out of the classroom. Bob Dylan says in "Mississippi,"

"You can always come back, but you can't come back all the way." Well, if you can't come back all the way, then you can't really come back at all. These prefaces I couldn't write had to be conceptualized as something else. I considered: if I had continued to write about the topic I had earlier passed by, then when I was all finished I might have created for this teacher a self-portrait in mosaic, a memoir in the form perhaps of graffiti, a travel book that recounted some of my journeying. And perhaps for *that* project I could use a preface. Thus, I offer here a rationalization for the appearance of *this* preface that is not exactly a preface: rather, it is a rationale that attempts to explain where in my failure I found success.

A Second Step: On an End to Beginnings and Endings

Of its origins as a word—and therefore a concept—I looked into my trusty Oxford English Dictionary (OED) and read that *preface* was a noun (*a* preface, late fourteenth century*)* before it became a verb (*to* preface, late seventeenth century), and originally the word had both a liturgical and secular meaning. In 1387, *a* preface referred to the introduction or prelude to the central part of the Eucharistic service and was comprised of an exhortation to thanksgiving and an offering of praise and glory to God; the preface concluded with the sanctus. A preface prepared the celebrant—made her spiritually ready—to partake in the sacred rite of the last supper that Jesus allowed would substitute for himself: "Here, this is my blood. Here this is my body." The preface prepared one to receive divinity. Now, I certainly respect my writing, but I never imagined it would lead anyone to any form of holiness.

For Jews, liturgically the P'sukei d'zimrah serves as a preface, though this service is not named so, as it is by Catholics. P'sukei d'zimrah are prayers of praise that precede the formal service; this particular preface ends with a formal call to communal prayer. For Jews, this preface represents an engagement in prayer to make prayer possible. In both Christian and Jewish senses, a preface serves as preparation for the main event. My preface to a series of prefaces would not *introduce* the book but would make the book—the sacred act—possible. It is always best to start at the beginning. I wrote, "I had set as my sabbatical project to write a series of prefaces." But now I was stuck. I had in mind only prefaces and no book. My preface prefaced nothing because I intended my prefaces as the main event! I continued to read in the OED.

In the previous year (1386), the word *preface* was attributed to Geoffrey Chaucer and referred to an introduction to a literary work; the preface usually contained some explanation of the work's subject, purpose, and scope, and provided some explanation of the method of treatment. It would seem that at one time the preface served the function of what today we might refer to as an introduction. However, today books sometimes contain both prefaces *and* introductions, and so I wondered about the actual nature of the prefaces that I had intended to write. My well-worn Thrall and Hibbard (thank you, Dr. Wise!) adds that a preface often "points out difficulties and uncertainties in connection with the writing of the book, and in general, informs the reader of such facts as [the author] thinks pertinent to a reading of the text" (1960, 374). Here the preface addresses the intent of the author more that it does the content of the book. The preface presents not the substance of the book but offers the reader insight into the process of its creation. Hence, the first words of the preface may note *its* beginning, but in fact the preface truly begins after the book ends. If the preface elaborates on the process undertaken in order to write the book, then the preface must be written last, after the book is finished.

But in the work that I had intended this to be, there was to be no book for which the preface would serve as preface, and hence, I could not say that *this* preface—that was originally meant to be a preface to a *series of prefaces*—begins or ends anything, except perhaps itself. And the failure of this preface suggested the necessary failure of the prefaces with which I intended to follow this preface: it and they would exist *sans* book. And so I considered: if I had no book for which *this* preface would serve as preface, then either I had no book at all or the book of a series of prefaces did not have to have either a beginning or an ending. This preface to what once was to have been a series of prefaces came into existence *in medias res*: it entered in the midst of my life that is thankfully not over; and the prefaces, now no longer prefaces because there was no book that would follow them, had become a series of not necessarily connected but certainly related explorations along some meandering brook that might at some point offer someone (even myself) opportunities for further exploration into education and the classroom (which are not necessarily identical) for as long as we breathe and think; and that what would connect these divergent and even disparate pieces would derive from the very life in the classroom that they revealed. The chapters that follow, then, represent some of the markers at which I have paused for various amounts of reason and time throughout my life, but from which, for any number of reasons and time, I have also moved. The book that follows this introductory piece represents a series of beginnings, but, unlike a preface, the book exists neither as nor at an end. The chapters will speak for themselves as beginnings, but since they are only beginnings with no book to follow, then they are also ends. This book is constituted as beginnings without ends and as endings without beginnings. This book, like me, enters *in media res*. I did not enter at the beginning but I was a beginning. Perhaps this book I write now begins as a book concerning endings and beginnings. It is a book about education! This preface is a beginning but it cannot tell you what it begins. Hence this preface is also an end because what follows doesn't belong to it. Let's say it's just part of the conversation.

On the Beginnings of Ends

The Good Witch Glinda has said that it is always best to start at the beginning, but the beginnings of any book are problematic. The idea of prefaces led me to consider the artificiality and arbitrariness of endings and beginnings: they do not, in fact, exist but are expediently created. The narrator in Anthony Trollope's novel *Barchester Towers* (1857, 2005) concludes his already lengthy story with the following extended apology:

> These leave takings in novels are as disagreeable as they are in real life; not so sad, indeed, for they want the reality of sadness, but quite as perplexing, and generally less satisfactory. What novelist . . . can impart an interest to the last chapter of his fictitious history? Promises of two children and superhuman happiness are of no avail nor assurance of extreme respectability carried to an age far exceeding that usually allotted to mortals. The sorrow of our heroes and heroines, they are your delight, oh public! Their sorrows, or their sins, or their absurdities; not their virtues, good sense, and consequent rewards. When we begin to tint our final pages with couleur de rose, as in accordance with fixed rule we must do, we altogether extinguish our own powers of pleasing. When we become dull we offend our intellect; and we must become dull or we should offend your taste . . . And who can apportion out and dovetail his incidents, dialogues, characters, and descriptive morsels, so as to fit them all exactly into 567 pages, without either compressing them unnaturally, or extending them artificially at the end of his labour? Do I not myself know that I am at this moment in want of a dozen pages, and that I am sick with cudgeling my brains to find them. And then when everything is done, the kindest-hearted critic of them all invariably twits us with the incompetency and lameness of our conclusion (p. 493).

Endings are impossible, Trollope says, because they put the quietus to events that really do not end: our lives may end, indeed, but not the events we have begun in our lives. Though death ends a life, it does not end Life; for the most part, we keep on keeping on. Thus, endings in novels are all artifice: we read to the end to learn how things turn out, but on the day following the novel's end everything might be changed. Indeed, it is often the reader's hope that they will have done so, and it is also true that this wished-for change may not necessarily be for the better. Often, Trollope says, we are dissatisfied with happy endings; readers prefer to read about sorrow and unhappiness because they make us feel better about our own lives. We prefer in our reading to keep company with those whose misery gives us comfort, and not with those whose good fortunes reveal us as the inadequate, unfortunate creatures we truly are. Writers write endings that satisfy our biddings. Endings that promise future delight remain unsatisfactory and inconclusive: we know from our pasts that things rarely, if ever, turn out the way we had planned. And when the novelist imposes the rose-colored filter over his narrative, the story pales.

In fact, endings are impossible and certainly unsatisfactory. For example, the last day of classes always makes me uncomfortable as I contemplate all that has not been finished; I am often troubled by how ineffectively I have even begun my task much less finished with it. The end of the class ought to be a beginning, but the final grade means to put an end to that beginning: if I have been truly effective in our work then at the end we teachers should have only just begun. Where is the end and where the beginning? Who can tell the dancer from the dance? There need be no preface because, Watson, the game is yet afoot.

I think that as endings are artifice, so too do beginnings lack credibility. Beginnings are defined mostly in retrospect and always arbitrarily. One enters Trollope's novel *in media res:* the action has long ago begun. Such is also the case with Laurence Sterne's *Tristram Shandy* (1980). The novel begins: "I wish my father or my mother, or indeed, both of them, as they were in duty both equally bound to it, had minded what they were about when they got me; had they duly consider'd how much depended on what they were doing" (p. 1). Tristram refers to the event of his conception, his ostensible beginning, and what is to my mind the most well-known instance of interrupted coitus: in the middle of the event Mrs. Shandy wondered to Mr. Shandy if he had remembered to wind the clock, an event that always coincided with the monthly fulfillment of his conjugal duties. As his wife knew the confluence of his ideas, in the midst of coitus she interrupted Mr. Shandy with the question concerning the winding of the clock! In such an environment was Tristram conceived, and that occasion, he avers, has made all the difference. Things are put in motion often by actions (or non-actions) over which we have no control, and we can never know where they might lead; the existence of a beginning is defined by the outcome, interestingly enough, by the arbitrary assignment of an ending. But my preface was going to serve as a beginning for which there would be no ending; or my preface was an end for which there had been no beginning. Beginnings are merely a step into the dark and we don't truly know where it is we stand. And though Tristram intends to narrate the story of his life starting from its auspicious beginnings, in fact he is not born until almost two hundred pages into the novel! A great deal occurs before his life begins.

Thus it is in the classroom. We all pretend that there are in them beginnings: the new year, or the new semester, a new class, a new unit, or even a new week promises to start all afresh. But, in fact, no one comes innocent into these spaces. The only blank slates to be written upon in these classrooms are the white chalk or smart boards that line the otherwise bare walls. The occupants of these places are already complex texts—neither beginnings nor endings—reluctant or willing participants in a complex continuing conversation for which no preface need be or even could be written. Today already contains yesterday and will be constructed with it; how will we tell the dancer from the dance? In the classroom, when did yesterday end and today begin? Here, when will today end and tomorrow begin? We call up background knowledge as preface to the presentation of new material, but what is called up, in fact, is only the teacher's agenda and wishes. Dewey notes: "Thinking is specific, in that different things suggest their own appropriate meanings, tell their own unique stories, and in that they do this in very different ways with different persons" (1910/1991, 39). How could one ever write a preface for such a diversity? Though, I regretfully acknowledge, it is true today that in schools, for the sake of efficiency and test scores, we make certain all are literally on the same page. Everyday must have its preface because everyone must know what the end of each day will be.

To continue with these speculations: I posit that the author composes the preface (a beginning) last but places it geographically and thematically first, making it an ending at the beginning. Paradoxically, the preface (a beginning) appears to be the end of a writer's work, though it does mark the beginning of the reader's engagement with it. The preface does not present an overview of the book—that apparently has become the function of the introduction—but informs the reader of the manner and the difficulty of the journey in which the writer has engaged in the writing and first reading of the very book the reader now holds and prepares to begin. Actually, the preface prepares the reader to read the book not by disclosing its subject but by introducing the presence of the author in the work. Neither beginning nor ending, the preface becomes an accompaniment or guide. Perhaps by mentioning the problems that the author overcame in the writing of the book, the writer imposes an implicit demand upon the reader that greater attention to the text be paid given the difficulties and extra effort the author undertook in the writing of it. Thus, like the teacher, the writer sets the objectives. The preface acknowledges the author's presence as celebrant and supplicant. I think that the stance I take in the classroom assumes that of a preface: participant and aspirant.

Now, not all books have prefaces though they all do begin nonetheless. Obviously, Chaucer knew about prefaces because the

OED attributes the introduction into the language of the word (and concept) officially to him, but I do not think he appended a preface onto the *Canterbury Tales*. Chaucer's *prologue* serves the purpose of a *preface:* sets the frame for the tales that will follow, though it does not refer to the composition of the tales themselves by a certain Geoffrey Chaucer. Rather, the prologue serves as an integral element in the text itself: it is meaningless without the tales even as the tales are adrift without the prologue. The prologue becomes part of the action. It is neither beginning nor ending though certainly it appears at the outset as rationale for the appearance of the text; the text can appear without the prologue and the prologue without the text but neither is complete without the other.

    Neither did Henry David Thoreau provide a preface to his *Walden,* the book itself, I think, constituting a preface, informing the reader of the manner and the difficulty of the journey in which the writer has engaged in the writing and first reading of the book the reader now holds and prepares to begin. *Walden* itself recounts the book's subject, purpose, scope, and method of treatment. All of *Walden* appears to be a preface, and the chapter "Reading" serves specifically for direction to how Thoreau's text ought to be read by addressing the author's own engagement in his reading of texts. And Walt Whitman, ever the iconoclast, in his preface to the 1855 edition of *Leaves of Grass* may have stylistically prepared the reader for the poems that followed but he certainly did not use his preface to thematically introduce the book or recount the difficulties he experienced in its writing. Whitman's preface actually celebrates the ideal American poet whom we might assume to be the author of *Leaves of Grass,* but the pronoun "I" does not appear in the entire preface nor is there mention made in the preface of the poems that follow it. Whitman's *preface* is more a manifesto than a beginning or an ending, and it might certainly be understood as a classical instance of hiding in plain sight. Most novels contain neither preface nor introduction, though

Henry James wrote long introductions to his revised works presenting in them his theories of fiction that would serve as guides for the reader.

Indeed, it strikes me now that only in *written* literature are prefaces prevalent. One might study *how* to look at a painting or listen to a particular piece of music, but the musician or artist does not offer, as part of the public presentation for any particular work, the context or conflict contained in its production as part of the work's presentation! Nor, I now consider, does one ever learn in school how to read a preface. All one is taught is that one must always start at the beginning, and then just follow the Yellow Brick Road!

But, as prefaces might be understood as advertisements for the author, then it might be fair to say that prefaces are autobiographies in disguise. They invite the reader into the text-proper by informing the reader of the book's features that the author has realized in its writing. Prefaces are not about the book but about the writer. They are essays: What else could an essay be but the author's exposure of his predilections? Wendy Leeser (1993, ix) describes an essay appropriate to the *Threepenny Review*: "as a piece of nonfiction prose that, while talking about something in the world at large, discusses and reveals the author's own personality as well . . . with the delicate evasiveness of a story." I had originally planned this book as a series of prefaces, but since I had not finished writing the book for which the writing was to have served as preface—indeed, I hadn't even started it!—then the existence of the preface became impractical if not impossible. Nonetheless, the topics of the proposed book for which I was supposed to be writing the prefaces were so intertwined in my life that the prefaces I had planned ceased to be so and became the main event and were transformed into essays that dealt as much with myself as with the subject. I found myself hiding in plain sight! Czeslaw Milosz (2002, 4), in the Introduction (a preface) to his autobiographical *Native Realm*, says, ". . . one can get at man only obliquely; only through the masquerade that is the extension of himself at a given moment, through his historical existence." There has been, he acknowledges, much to see along the way. And so now, with my companions, the tin man with his heart, and the scarecrow with his brain, the lion with his courage, I sit here writing what was to be a preface to my series of prefaces but that has now become a prefatory essay to a series of essays exploring some of the emotional and physical adventures I have experienced in and out of the classroom on my way to the Emerald City to seek the Wizard of Oz. What follows began intellectually as prefaces but transformed in the writing into memoirist essays because when we speak in the essay we speak not only about the subject at hand but also about ourselves. Or as Hamlet says about the play before the king: by indirection to find direction out.

When does a book begin if not at the beginning? In what has become a very famous letter (published without the permission of its sender), Ralph Waldo Emerson wrote to Whitman concerning the first edition of *Leaves of Grass*, a copy of which the young poet had sent to the famous seer and essayist. Emerson wrote: "I greet you at the beginning of a great career, which yet must have had a long foreground somewhere, for such a start." The idea of the long foreground belies the very idea of a beginning; I do not know when a foreground, in fact, begins or how one might be even properly defined. So with this book: it might have a start but it lacks a beginning. As for its long foreground: that must be my life! If in the preface to his autobiography Henry Adams (1961, xxiii) announces his purpose to discover "what part of education has, in his personal experience, turned out to be useful, and what not," he discovers (or does he conclude?) in the writing that his education turned out to be not at all useful except to reveal its ineffectiveness. The book concludes: "The attempt of the American of 1900 to educate the American of 2000, must be even blinder than that of the Congressman of 1800, except so far as he had learned his ignorance" (497). If in the preface Adams asks what value his education has had, then the autobiography is the answer. And this answer defines the character of the writer! Interestingly, Michel de Montaigne uses the preface to his book of essays to disclaim any purpose to the writing of it. His preface is a disclaimer. "I have set myself no goal but a domestic and private one. I have had no thought of serving either you or my own glory . . ." (2003, 2). Montaigne's preface, written after the text that follows it, announces the non-existence of the book! At the end of the preface, Montaigne actually bids the reader goodbye, his preface now a bidding adieu: "So farewell," he concludes, even as the essays begin. Montaigne's preface serves as the departure of the writer and a beginning to the essays, but indeed, the preface promises that in the essays that follow "I want to be seen here in my simple, natural, ordinary fashion, without straining or artifice; for it is myself that I portray." Even as he said goodbye, Montaigne would say hello.

It would seem that having experienced a bout of depression in his time, prior to the advent of psychotropic drugs—Montaigne says that by "the gloom of the solitude into which I had cast myself some years ago"—he had undertaken to remedy his condition by meddling in writing. That is, Montaigne would write himself into mental health. Modestly declaring that he really did not know very much and therefore was devoid of material about which to write, "I presented myself to myself for argument and subject." The preface to the *Essays* both prefaces and apologizes for the book's matter: that he would be both the subject of his book and its author. "I am myself the matter of my book," Montaigne warns his reader, "you would be unreasonable to spend your leisure on so frivolous and vain a subject." The preface announces the subject and process and then dismisses it and discourages the reader from attending to the text at all! Montaigne's preface is truly an ending. But not really: as he aged Montaigne continued to revise the essays that his preface had discounted as frivolous. As his life grew so too did his essays. Hence, his preface really announces the end of the beginning and the beginning of the end.

Montaigne's text is not an autobiography however, in the more formal sense, for though it is himself about which he writes, he does so through discussion of those things that interest him and about which he wishes to contemplate. And since the essays show Montaigne, as he is well aware, hiding in plain sight, for the sake of modesty he has made sure that in the essays he is seen fully clothed! Had he lived in a more temperate climate, he says, in a freer and more natural society, he admits, he would have portrayed himself unclothed and naked. But in the present state of culture and climate, such an exposure would have been inappropriate and unwise. Interestingly, Montaigne introduces a metaphor not too far from that chosen by Henry Adams whose book records the education—the clothes—with which his society has adorned him, even as Montaigne prefigures Philip Roth's motives for his autobiography. In *The Facts: A Novelist's Autobiography,* Roth (1988, 5) writes to his fictional creation, Zuckerman, in what could only be termed a preface, "Here, so as to fall back into my former life, to retrieve my vitality, to transform myself into myself, I began rendering experience untransformed." He, too, would write himself back to health! As in any good preface, Roth explores the problems he had to confront—and that still confront him—about the writing of the book. Roth (10) wonders to Zuckerman, "Is the book any good? Because *The Facts* has meant more to me than may be obvious and because I've never worked before without my imagination having been fired by someone like you or Portnoy or Tarnopol or Kepesh. I'm in no real position to tell." Roth's preface both explains and questions the work.

Nonetheless, Montaigne, Adams, and Roth have hit upon a strategy with which I have much sympathy: to find themselves in the writing *in medias res.* Disclaiming method, Montaigne (2003, 31) argues in the essay "Of Prompt or Slow Speech" for the necessity for both forms of discourse. Montaigne asserts, "I find myself more by chance encounter than by searching my judgment." That is, by prompt, spontaneous speech Montaigne will tender some thought that may (or may not) have relevance: only in conversation—in relationship—will the sense bear fruit. "I will have tossed off some subtle remark as I write (I mean, of course, dull for anyone else, sharp for me . . .). Later I have lost the point so thoroughly that I do not know what I meant; and sometimes a stranger has discovered it before I do." Indeed, as Adams suggests that his own mistakes will only be known in the light of the mistakes of others (which is the topic of his autobiography), and as Roth wonders to his intimate, Zuckerman, about the quality of his book, so does Montaigne suggest that only in the reading can sense be made: "If I erased every passage where this happens to me, there would be nothing left of myself. At other times, chance will show the light clearer than noonday and make me astonished at my hesitations." Montaigne, Adams, and Roth depend on the future reader for discovery. Their writing is all autobiography and therefore, of dubious credibility: their prefaces announce this caution, but their prefaces are neither beginnings nor endings. At best, they are inculpatory evidence.

So with me . . . "Thus reader, I am myself the matter of my book." I had thought originally to locate myself by these series of prefaces. These prefaces would have revealed some of the places I had once briefly paused and even considered for a time to settle, but then the school bell rang and I was due in class; I became distracted and moved on. Nevertheless, these seemingly disparate locations have had substantial influence on my path, especially when I thought about the beauty of the way and the goodness of the wayfarers. If I could not write the prefaces for books I had not written *because* I had not written them, I thought that at least I could, in some leisure, revisit those places; return for even a short time to my earlier manifestations of desire. If Abraham never did get to the land that God meant to show to him, there is still in the writing a detailed map of his wanderings. I will, in the prefaces-now-become-essays that follow, chart some of the details of my journey. Not a nostalgic musing in old photographs pasted in a worn, dusty album, but an energetic recounting, not unlike the recounting of the Israelites' history since the Exodus that Moses offers in *Deuteronomy*, arriving finally at the charge to "Choose Life—if you and your offspring would live." These essays recount my journey through the wilderness—some of where I lived and what I lived for—and my choice of life. These essays recover and project.

Montaigne wrote his essays as self-therapy; they restored him to peace by allowing him to construct in them his sense of order out of his feelings of chaos. Montaigne writes "that in order to contemplate [the] ineptitude and strangeness [of his thoughts] I have begun to put them in writing, hoping in time to make my mind ashamed of itself" (2003, 25). When one is idle one is quiet and at some kind of rest. One waits expectantly. And so I would consider that Montaigne's writing would be not a distraction from life but the activity in life to which his desire led. In fact, the writing that arose out of the state of his idleness returned him to that which most concerned him: his immediate or insistent matters. Montaigne's essays concern his many attachments to the things of this world.

Many of us distract ourselves to avoid the chimeras and fantastic monsters; hence the focus on objectives in the classroom, perhaps. But Montaigne used his writing to engage with and to domesticate these imagined threats. In the conclusion to *Walden*, Thoreau implores his reader: "Nay, be a Columbus to whole new continents and worlds within you, opening new channels, not of trade, but of thought. Every man is the lord of a realm beside which the earthly empire of the Czar is but a petty state, a hummock left by the ice." I have aspired to this ideal in my life, and have been content to move forward in the realization though never to fully achieve it. I rule a kingdom of thought, and I lord over dozens of books still to be read and papers unfinished that await attention; I maintain fields of thought demanding cultivation and harvest.

Thoreau argues with intense feeling that the great work of the individual in this world should be self-study—to journey inward to discover, if not the source of our being, then at least to learn of that being's use, and for this voyage to load our cargo holds with tins of preserved meats, if necessary, for what else, he demands, are meats preserved! Thoreau means for us to live not on the surface of life, but to sound the depths of our bottomless Waldens. Thoreau cautions that to concern our selves with the petty details of the world ("It is enough to read one newspaper a week," he advises) to the exclusion of study leading to self-awareness is to forfeit the greater exploration for the sake of the lesser one. Such a choice would keep us always on the very lowest road. Certainly the crude politics and power mongering of the contemporary United States are exemplars of this greatest lesser.

For Thoreau, as for Montaigne, Adams, and Roth, our responsibility in this life is to know our selves, and I believe that that knowledge includes a keen and critical awareness of our place in the world. As did Marx from the other side of the world, Thoreau argued that most importantly we must own ourselves, and that this accomplishment derives from a self-knowledge that might prevent a life of servitude and quiet desperation. People may make their own history, but not in the circumstances of their choosing: we must learn our circumstances to understand our freedom. Even if our lives *be* mean, knowledge of that meanness might provide us with some enlightenment and element of control. Perhaps our complicated conversations are all prefaces—stories of the processes and difficulties in which we engage as we write ourselves. We place these artificial beginnings about our artificial ends.

So perhaps this little essay serves as instructional details in which my experience of writing the text informs the reader for what to read in it. This is what I have learned while I engaged in the writing of this book, the author's preface says. This book is about schooling and education. I have spent my entire life in schools as student, teacher, and professor: What is't I do? What is to be done?

I had thought it appropriate to add a preface to what was to have been my series of prefaces because . . . well, I had to begin somewhere! I wondered: How do I start for the Emerald City? It's always best to start at the beginning—and all you do have to do is follow the Yellow Brick Road. Ah, but it wasn't that easy, and one road leads sometimes to two, and as Robert Frost knew, when *two* roads—yellow or not—diverge in a yellow wood, one must choose which to follow, and that choice will make all the difference.

There is a play tonight before the king that might unkennel his occulted guilt. These essays, reader, are my thoughts that remain below.

Chapter 2

Why Read the Book?

Why Read?

I WAS HAVING A CONVERSATION AT THE LOCAL COFFEE SHOP this past week with my friend, Reuven. He reads books, and after opening pleasantries—"How are you?" ("Fine. And you?"); "What's new?" ("Ah, not much. And with you?"); "Watch the game?" ("No, I'm not a big sports fan!")—we talk about books, and in the course of that discussion, other aspects of our lives inevitably open. I know that what and how we read are topics intimately reflective of our personal lives, and that to talk about our choices of reading revealingly opens a window onto our intimacies. And though I recognize that as we are certainly more than what we eat, and I acknowledge that we are more than what we read, I have been considering that there is an intimate connection between our reading and our selves, and that what rests on a person's bookshelf (metaphorical and otherwise) tells a significant story about the character of that person. When I inquire, "What are you reading?" I also ask, "Tell me who you might now be and are in the process of becoming." "Camerado!" Walt Whitman calls to me in his poem "So Long": "This is no book. Who touches this touches a man." Reading engages us in relationships, and we are always changed by these intimacies. And I believe that it is also true that to touch the man or woman is also to understand what books he or she touches. To touch oneself is to touch the book that is held. I am writing a book about some of the books I have touched. Who touches this book touches a man.

I am a reader: there are always several books open about the premises. In my cabin office lie ready the academic books to be studied during the daylight hours: books of philosophy and psychology, of pedagogy and history, of theories of science, literature, art, and the like. These are the books that feed my intellect and that inspire my own speculative writing. I purport to be a scholar, and sometimes I even behave like one. I have learned to love these books and the struggle they demand: when I read these texts I feel powerful, and like the Incredible Hulk grow huge and burst out of the seams of my consciousness. And in the house proper, on the tables by the fireplace (gas, not wood-burning), lining the shelves that cover the walls throughout the house, resting invitingly on the night table beside my bed and in the stands by the toilets, lying about the floors waiting to be raised up, are the novels and dramas that feed my soul. It is in them that I discover people living, and in the reading I share in their experiences to better understand my own.

Some of my dearest friends and comrades are the books that sit on these shelves. I call them friends because with them I have shared a precious intimacy. They are my chosen, and I have given my life to them. I have stood naked with them and I have written my secrets on their souls; in return, they have offered me their private thoughts and given me entrance to their most intimate confidences. I have lain with these friends during my brightest days and my darkest nights; in the lonely moments of my soul they have comforted me and been my companions through until morning. These friends and I have together laughed and wept, bemoaned and celebrated our individual states and that of the world; we have together in joy studied and frolicked. These friends have drunk with me my coffees and liquors—I have stained their pages with my carelessness, and they have often served as loyal valets and wiped my face when I was too untidy. These intimates have entered the cloistered spaces into which even my children have no access; they have suffered without complaint the stench of my ordure and enjoyed the sweeter smells of my private fragrances. The books have kept the splatter from my desktops and my lap, and screened my face from the muck and mire of the world; they have sometimes even borne the blows aimed at me.

Like me, my friends have aged, and sometimes when I pull one out from the shelf and beg some companionship, its fragility becomes all too evident. The glue has irrevocably dried up; the covers slip off and the pages detach from the spine. With the slightest movement, pages float down like leaves off the trees in autumn—or drift through the air like souls lost. Sometimes when I pull out a volume to renew some familiarity or to enter into some new intimacy, the book comes undone in my arms and becomes unreadable. I fear I can no longer enter into new conversations with this particular friend, for it can no longer bear the weight of my body or my soul. My pens and pencils have rent the lines and spaces; my own voices engraved in the pages have become faded in their memory.

What shall I do with these hoary books? Haven't I now chosen you, and how shall I forsake thee? I hold one up and it crumbles in my hands. Delicately I embrace the volume and gently turn some pages: I see along the margins shadowy words in a familiar handwriting, and in the present reconsider some thoughts that contain some of my past. Without these books I would have no access to that past. I hold onto these friends for my life. The shelves bend under their weight. Who touches this book touches a man!

Jeanette Winterson (2011, 42) says, "Fiction and poetry are doses, medicines. What they heal is the rupture reality makes on the imagination." I am skeptical of her definition of these literatures: for me, Winterson posits an imagination that exists *a priori to* any contact we make with an external world against which our imagination conflicts. I do not perceive the world, but I do perceive *my* world and it is my imagination that constructs and orders that world. My imagination *derives* from my engagement in the world, an engagement that begins at birth, and my imagination develops in the space that exists between my unknowable Desire and the world in which my Desire must be fulfilled. I may know my imagination through its products that become available to thought and sensual delight, but my Desire I will never know: if I knew my Desire, then I think what I felt would be not Desire but appetite, and I could then seek directly its satisfaction. Desire is what sends Abraham from his home in Ur to a land he does not know. Desire is perhaps what drives Eustacia Vye out onto the moors, and it is, perhaps, her Desire that Holden Caulfield so admires about her: he possesses Desire of his own. Desire inspires us to action or it drives us mad: I think here of Pip in *Moby Dick* (Melville, 1962), who fell into the wondrous depths of the sea "where strange shapes of the unwarped primal world glided to and fro before his passive eyes . . . He saw God's foot upon the treadle of the loom, and spoke it; and therefore his shipmates called him mad." Who can see God and live? But to seek out from our Desire in the world through our imagination enacts our creativity, and reading is a creative act, evoking both the text and ourselves. John Berger (2011), speaking of the impulse to draw, says that we draw to make something visible that demands to be made visible—but what that something is we do not know until it is seen, and when we bring that something to its proper destination we will know when we have arrived there. I believe this is as true for writing and reading as it is for drawing. When we read, we find something we did not know to look for because we had not known it had been even lost. My books offer me a world I cannot immediately experience but that I immediately seek; the books give my Desire some fulfillment. My imagination grows and strengthens. Reality does not rupture my imagination but comes to substance through it.

My readings send me out into the world: as the reader I read out from my curiosity, even as the writer I write out from it. I discover a great book when what the author is curious about elaborates on that about which I am curious, or when the author's curiosity stimulates my own and opens new perspectives on my world. My imagination grows and my reality deepens. I am as much interested in *how* a book satisfies my Desire—how it adds to my imagination—and what the book reveals about me to myself as I am interested in what the book might mean. Ever the stoic, I believe that reality is what I get for being alive. Reading is essential to my living really. Reality is the sometimes-cold and sometimes-hot walk out to the cabin where I create something I do not yet know but soon will discover. And if that travel out be neither hot nor cold, it is nonetheless a walk and requires attention and effort. Seneca (2004, 183) writes, "So the spirit must be trained to a realization and an acceptance of its lot. . . . We've entered into a world in which these are the terms life is lived on . . ." Or as Dylan might say, "It's life and life only." Books explore those terms of life in which I have (and will have) interest.

For example, I have long been interested in what Hamlet calls "the slings and arrows of outrageous fortune." I—and so many others—wonder, "Why me?" Philip Roth's book *Nemesis* (2010) gives me pause. The novel takes place during the polio epidemic in New Jersey in 1944 and for me addresses (among other things) issues of agency, responsibility, and fate. Nemesis, a female goddess in Greek mythology, was the spirit of divine retribution directed at those who suffer from hubris: the assumption of too much belief in their human capacity to control events. Today, nemesis refers to an archenemy, as Lex Luthor was Superman's enemy, or the Joker serves as Batman's, or the Republican Party as mine. Nemesis serves as a check (and often a checkmate) to one's authority. Nemesis is not fate but she may appear to be fate to those who in their unchecked pride maintain a belief in their absolute power to control events and themselves. Nemesis punctures that pride, and I think that it is in response to Nemesis that one's character becomes clear. It is certainly so in this novel. I think it might be true for my life as well.

Bucky Cantor, a young gym teacher at a local elementary school in the Newark, New Jersey area, is hired as playground coordinator in the Weequahic section of the city at the conclusion of the school year. For the boys and children home for the summer and out of school—not away at summer camp—Cantor is to organize and supervise recreational activities. In his stature and his actions, Bucky—Mr. Cantor, as the narrator of the first section refers to him—serves as the boys' hero. It is he to whom they look for organization, direction, and control. Around Bucky the boys feel safe. The year is 1944 and, because Bucky must wear corrective lenses for his seriously strained eyesight, he has received a 4F from his draft board and become exempt from service in the military during World War II. His two college friends, Jake and Dave, are both overseas and fighting in the invasion of France during the Normandy offensive. Bucky is devastated by his inability to serve in the war, almost ashamed to have remained states side, but he approaches his job with an energy and determination that can only be admired. At first, all that Bucky must handle is the normal energy of adolescent boys and girls and the horrible heat that oppresses the area. But then, suddenly, the occasional case of polio escalates into an epidemic, and Bucky's ranks are soon shrunken by the onslaught of the disease. *His* boys become sick and some of them die.

Throughout the epidemic Bucky remains remarkably calm; he visits the families of the boys who succumbed, and is often the target of their vitriol—in their grief it is he they blame for allowing the boys to play so hard during the oppressive heat of the summer—calumny which he accepts with patience and equanimity. Bucky manages the uncomfortable presence of Horace, the local cognitively disabled man, and he protects the boys, many if not all of them Jewish, from the invasion of ten young Italian men who assert that they are delivering the polio virus to the Jewish section! When they spit all over the ground, planting the polio germs on the sweltering concrete, Bucky orchestrates the peaceful departure of the Italian boys, and then has his charges clean the sidewalk with hot water and ammonia, as if the Italians had indeed left behind the polio and that under Bucky's direction they could cleanse away the infection. Bucky consults with his girlfriend's father, Dr. Steinberg, who assures him that though the epidemic seems harsh, it is no worse than a previous appearance in 1916 (during another war) and that he is doing the right thing by his boys. He calms Bucky's fears, and alleviates his concern that the world is operated by a cruel God, or even that there is, in fact, no God at all! Bucky Cantor returns to his own charges and assuages their fears with his gained knowledge and his presumed power. He serves as the boys' hero.

But, when given a chance to escape the oppressive city, Bucky leaps and takes a job as a waterfront director at a camp in the Poconos where Marcia, his girlfriend and soon to be fiancé, serves as counselor. There, amidst the green and fresh air, life seems perfect—until the first case of polio strikes a counselor in Bucky's bunk. And then the disease afflicts several other campers as well as Marcia's younger sister, and then finally polio strikes Bucky himself. And upon discovering that he is infected, Bucky interprets himself as the germ, the infection that has corrupted not only the boys on the playground but the paradise in the Poconos, and his pride refuses to accept that he is only another victim and not the cause of the epidemic. Bucky's nemesis is not polio but the pride in his belief that he has been the carrier of the plague that originally infected the playground of Weequahic and now afflicts the idyllic setting of Indian Hills. Bucky's pride presumes a world where Bucky is able to control events, and his unwillingness to accept this lack of control destroys his life. He becomes his own nemesis. When he asks "Why me?" Bucky assumes that he ought not to be vulnerable, and that he is invincible. He couldn't have been more wrong.

We ignore the contingent—those slings and arrows of outrageous fortune—at the expense of our lives, and to ignore the contingent is to relinquish whatever small control we yet retain in this world. But the contingent, by definition, exists so far from our control that we would relievedly dismiss it from our consciousness. Despite Bucky's limp, it is Bucky's seeming invincibility that remains the lasting image of him for Arnie Mesnikof, one of Bucky's boys, from that summer: "Running with the javelin aloft, stretching his throwing arm back behind his body, bringing the throwing arm through to release the javelin high over his shoulder—and releasing it then like an explosion—he seemed to us invincible" (p. 280). But it was all illusion. Alas, he wasn't. Nor was Arnie, who himself had contracted polio during that horrible summer. Nor, I consider, am I. My head remains bloody but unbowed. Reading shines such light on reality as to make it appear anew to me. I am changed by *Nemesis* in ways I have yet to learn.

For me, books are where I go not for melioration but for stimulation; books provide me insight into my imagination from my experience in reality, and offer me insight into reality from the experience of my imagination. I enter my books in search of that which my reality doesn't readily reveal to me, and I give to the reality of the books the resources of my imaginative life that includes even that which remains below the conscious level. I come out of the book changed. I have long trusted that every book I read serves as a piece of the great puzzle that I construct as some picture of my world and my place in it. I am never sure of what the whole picture might finally consist, but I do not doubt that the enterprise of puzzle-making will be completed at the moment of my death and then the whole will be known, albeit a bit late. To the books I bring the life I have lived and thought, and it is from these books that I go back changed to the world of reality. I live richly in the books and I live richer from them. When I have nothing to read I become disoriented and vulnerable: I see no pattern at all in the puzzle. Without a book I feel lost: not knowing what next to read results from not knowing what world I want next to enter: it is a symptom that I am too unsettled in the world in which I now reside. I become restless, anxious, and unfocused, and reading requires a commitment to enter into a world that requires determined attention.

And so I ask Reuven, "What are you reading now?" The question is this pedagogue's opening move in ways not unlike the therapist's inquiry, "So, what's going on?" Reuven informs me that he has undertaken a project to read, in a single year, books from A to Z: that is, over the course of one year, he will choose his reading (this year, only novels) by the initial letter of the author's last name. Employing *some* critical discrimination, general curiosity, and autobiographical excavation—he does not simply wander to an alphabetic section and pull down the first book he sees—Reuven will choose his next book by the initial letter of the author's name, though he also does not commit himself to making his choice in strict alphabetical order. Nevertheless, the choice is not fortuitous: there is Desire (albeit unacknowledged) behind any particular choice. Reuven is a reader: stacked high about his home are books (mostly novels) that he has acquired at various used book stores (his favorite venue for such purchases), and he appears at most social events with a paperback stuffed into his back pocket in the event that a spare moment would materialize in which he might continue his engagement with the book. For the present, Reuven's reading selections are made in some artificial linear order: he will read any book he pleases as long as the author's last name begins with a letter he has not yet read, and he has vowed not to read any single author twice. His choice is determined strictly by the alphabet, though I recognize that behind this venture is some unknowable Desire that drives not just this entire enterprise but the particular book choice of the present as well. That is why he is reading in the first place!

I suggest to him that it would seem (to me, at least) that his reading differs little from most random reading: he rejects a book not by its cover, or even by its subject, but by the initial letter of the author's last name. He laughs, and in reply says that there is, indeed, order in his disorder and not mere arbitrariness. I ask him if he ever thought to have the opportunity and pleasure to read a second novel by an author whose current read intrigues him to no end. He throws up his hands with his palms faced upward, shrugs his shoulders, and again laughs heartily (and how I love that laugh): "I'll read that later, when I've finished this project." Reuven is a reader, and his present method is one example of how one may choose what to read next. Really there is no end to his interest—but it must be driven by some Desire. I ask him what he intends to do when he has arrived at the end of the alphabet, and he shrugs his shoulders and laughs. "I don't know. But I'm not concerned. I'll think of something." Actually, he has already begun to plan: next year he will embark on a project to read only non-fiction history texts, working backwards through the decades until he arrives at an historical moment when reading by centuries makes more sense.

How we choose our reading is my concern here because, as I have said, to know what book she holds offers insight into she who holds the book. Of course, I refer here to people who continue to read books, though it is also true that not to read books goes some way towards aspects of self-definition! If we go to school—and by law most of us do so until at least the age of sixteen—then, for the most part, the books from which we are taught to read and that we end up reading are chosen for us (though many—with announced pride—survive high school, alas, without reading a book!) As a high school English teacher, I was one of those who mandated the reading of assigned texts; this choice texts was almost always ideologically based in someone's definition of "literature" (sometimes even mine!), and established some criteria for what will count as "good" reading.

The bookrooms of the schools are filled with such texts, with some of those rooms, alas, more replete than others. When I went to school, except for Edith Wharton's *Ethan Frome,* I recall very little that we were assigned to read that had not been written by white males, most of whom were dead. Concerning *Ethan Frome* we did not study Lionel Trilling's thrilling (my judgment) essay on moral inertia in Wharton's novel. In "The Morality of Inertia," Trilling argues that "moral inertia, the *not* making of moral decisions, constitutes a large part of the moral life of humanity" (2000, 337). Morality is simply what one does and not necessarily what one chooses to do, and that the morality of inertia—doing without thinking—leads easily to the immorality of inertia. I learned that I would do well to consider what it is I do. I discovered Trilling's essay when I was teaching *Ethan Frome* from a school bookroom still filled with the work of mostly male authors whose skin was white and whose lives had mostly ended. In my memoirs, I think I might trace my interest in ethics to Trilling's essay, pretending that such a direct line exists.

Nor was much different in the choice of texts I was assigned and that I read in college: I was educated in the school of new criticism, a literary lens invented by white males, at least in part to preserve the world they desired to value even if the reality of the world in which they actually lived denied them this opportunity. We read from the canon, works that had been written for the most part by white European males, then (and now still) deceased, with an occasional gesture to Emily Dickinson and George Eliot. My reading offered me portraits of a troubled and homogenized world with a neurotic and homogenized populace; of difference I knew very little and had much to learn.

First, however, I had to learn the joy of choosing to read from an unknowable Desire, an active imagination, and a demanding reality. I do not mean to address here the fierce debate over the successes and failures of various philosophies of reading instruction in the United States over the years. The subject of my 1994 book, *Occupied Reading,* concerned the pedagogies of reading in public schools. That work was a scholarly attempt at politics and polemics: I argued that if reading occurred in the process of actual living and viable need, then reading might cease being a strictly pedagogical concern and become an essential practice. In my book I sought to place the current debate in reading instruction in some historical, political, and psychological context that I hoped might affect what I believed was the misdirection that reading pedagogy had taken in the United States over the past several centuries. *Occupied Reading* did not acquire much readership, alas.

I recognize that there are communities that exist in the United States that cannot maintain a bookstore and whose libraries are woefully ill-funded and ill-used. Literacy, of course, remains a complex economic, social, and political issue. As for me, when I enter a bookstore today, the enormous quantity of books on the shelves suggests that there must be somewhere a huge community of readers out there for which a huge community of writers are writing; or else it is the case that a great deal of paper and ink is going to waste. And though literacy has remained a contentious issue in the politics of education in the United States, it is not actually literacy with which I am presently concerned when I speak of reading. I do not wish to re-engage in that debate here. What I am interested in at present is the manner and motives of those who *do* read and who *choose* the books to be read. And I believe that the answer to this query remains a question: we choose our reading to answer a question that has been posed to us. As Thoreau (1960) says,

> I long ago lost a hound, a bay horse, and a turtle dove, and am still on their trail. Many of the travellers I have spoken concerning them, describing their tracks and what calls they answered to. I have met one or two who had heard the hound and the tramp of the horse, and even seen the dove disappear behind a cloud, and they seemed as anxious to recover them as if they had lost them themselves.

We read out from our lives, and then from the books we return inevitably changed to those lives. Though our Desire is no more known, it is yet more visible.

For me, reading has been an unquestioned but questioning compulsion throughout my life. My mother used to adore telling others how I would run to her (to *her*, of course!) with a book held out in my hands and cry, "Read to me, read to me!" I cannot say what led me to books in the first place, though I now suspect that it was the opportunity to be held in her lap whilst she read. Perhaps books were the means to receive warmth and attention. I don't know, in fact, but certainly I believe that every child deserves a lap in which to sit and to be read to by someone. Reading was the activity that expressed love, I think. I must have sensed, too, that in these books there was a land to which I could go and that with effort could be mine. Books fed my imagination even as it deepened my reality. Winterson (who, like my friend Reuven, also chose to read English Literature A–Z) writes in her memoir *Why Be Normal When You Can Be Happy?* (2011, 117), "Reading things that are relevant to the facts of your life is of limited value. The facts are, after all, only the facts, and the yearning passionate part of you will not be met there. That is why reading ourselves as a fiction as well as fact is so liberating." In the novels and poetry and short stories she reads, Winterson can study the emotional and imaginative complex responses to life that are not fact but fiction, but that yet might be immediately relevant to her life. From my adult perspective, from *her* adult perspective, that motive satisfies my question.

Though I must admit to some discomfort with an author's use in autobiography or memoir of the second and third person self-referential pronouns, as does Winterson when she states how reading facts is of little value to "your" life. I think that this custom is a normalizing ploy that pins me to the author's consciousness and defines me as identical to the author; or else it is a narrative self-alienating device that presumes a measure of objectivity (as in Paul Auster's *Winter Journal*); or else it becomes a mask to assume an invisibility, as in Salman Rushdie's *Joseph Anton: A Memoir*. I resent the tactic. *Mea culpa:* I have too often written in the third person plural pronoun to hide in its crowd. Nevertheless, I do tend to agree with Winterson (which is why I have written her words in my journal) that facts offer me little insight into my life. My life is not the concatenation of facts, but it becomes, instead, the responses to the events I refer to as facts. Reading awakens my responses, and when all goes well it calls up emotions and feelings I had forgotten that I remembered. Winterson (2011, 162) writes, "We bury things so deep we no longer remember there was anything to bury. Our bodies remember. Our neurotic states remember. But we don't." Now, I prefer not to separate my body from my self, and I discount the presence of some homunculus that assumes the task of concealing that which we prefer not to view. I like to think that we are always our neurotic states. Czeslaw Milosz (1968, 185) writes in his memoir, *Native Realm*, "Certain periods of our lives are difficult to remember. They are like the jumbled dreams out of whose obscure depths only one or two details emerge clearly. This means we have not mastered our material and insofar as the past is at all decipherable—have not deciphered its hidden contents." Milosz and Winterson suggest to me that it is only hubris that fools me into believing that I remain, in my knowledge, in full control of my life and that leads me to trust the facts as my sole resource for understanding my self and my world. In "The Hedgehog and the Fox," Isaiah Berlin (2000, 488) explores Tolstoy's theory of history as it is evidenced in *War and Peace*—a theory with which I think Berlin has great sympathy. Berlin says that Tolstoy acknowledges that

> we are all immersed and submerged in a medium that, precisely to the degree to which we inevitably take it for granted as part of ourselves, we do not and cannot observe as if from the outside; cannot identify, measure and seek to manipulate, cannot even be

wholly aware of, too closely interwoven with all that we are and do to be lifted out of the flow . . . and observed with scientific detachment, as an object. It—the medium in which we are—determines our more permanent categories, our standards of truth and falsehood, and the peripheral, of the subjective and the objective of the beautiful and the ugly, of movement and rest, of past, present and future, of one and many; hence, neither these, nor any other explicitly conceived categories or concepts, can be applied to it . . .

The facts offer limited knowledge. Tolstoy was aware of the "sheer, *de facto* difference which divides and forces which disrupt the human world, [and was] utterly incapable of being deceived by the many subtle devices, the unifying systems and faiths and sciences, by which the superficial and desperate sought to conceal the chaos from themselves and from one another" (2007, 497). Literature offers to me an alternative perspective to that which the facts and rationality present. Milosz (1968) says, "It is enough that we realize to what extent thought and word are incommensurable with reality. Then it is possible to set one's limits consciously." So much depends upon a red wheelbarrow. To know for sure is to surely not know. In Roth's *The Human Stain* (2000), Nathan Zuckerman furtively observes Faunia and Coleman at a concert and intuits that Coleman had told Faunia, his lover, the great secret he has trusted to no one else. Zuckerman writes: "How do I know she knew? I don't. I couldn't know that either. I can't know. Now that they're dead, nobody can know. For better or worse, I can only do what everyone does who think they know. I imagine. I am forced to imagine. It happens to be what I do for a living. It is my job" (p. 213). So is it with me: I am driven to the book by not knowing, for though I know I cannot know, I can imagine. To imagine is why I read.

These writers suggest to me that facts are only the smallest part of the story: what are called facts may appear to be what happened but are not what was meant or intended. And since we can never know the end result of a fact any more than we can ever truthfully narrate our death and write out our life until its end, then all that we do when we read is narrate from and to our autobiography even when that narration masquerades as cool presentation of fact. The facts are always deficient. Roth (1988, 272) has expressed a similar idea earlier in his text, *The Facts: A Novelist's Autobiography*. Roth asks Zuckerman, his character and therefore the person who should best know Roth, to read his autobiography in manuscript and to offer, perhaps, some constructive criticism, and Zuckerman responds that the manuscript is not at all worth publishing: it is, Zuckerman accuses, a fake. "Even if it's no more than one percent that you've edited out, that's the one percent that counts—the one percent that's saved for your imagination and that changes everything. . . ." The bare facts are too bare. Winterson (2011, 8) says something similar about her first novel: "Mrs. Winterson objected to what I had put in, but it seemed to me that what I had left out was the story's silent twin." So, too, with our readings: I think we read and attend to the silences in the books and in our lives. We read and fill the empty margins. For Roth, as it must be for Winterson, fiction opens the world of the self, but we must first learn to read and to discover ourselves in the language and the silences of others.

There is something in the book to which I viscerally respond: that is the experience of emotion. I name that response and I experience feeling. To touch this book touches a man. Reading starts with a question and the response begins in the body. Speaking about himself in the second person, Auster (2012, 68) says, "Whenever you come to a fork in the road, your body breaks down, for your body has always known what your mind doesn't know, and however it chooses to break down, whether with mononucleosis or gastritis or panic attacks your body has always borne the brunt of your fears and inner battles, taking the blows your mind cannot or will not stand up to." And then the mind can function. Two roads always diverge in a yellow wood, and when Frost says, "and I—I took the one less traveled by," I think he depicts that moment when emotion—that body response—becomes feeling—that moment when he and I assume a new consciousness and become a new entity. I am reminded of the moment when the Israelites had heard God's commandments from Moses and the people respond, "Naaseh v'nishma"—"We will do and we will hear" (Exodus 24:8). First they will respond and then they will understand. Spinoza says that I cannot change my mind without changing my body, and that I cannot know my mind except through a change in my body. "For the mind does not know itself, except in so far as it perceived the ideas of the modifications of body." (1955, Prop XXIX—Corollary). I read another book.

And perhaps Winterson is also correct when she says that in the reading and the writing—the writer is always the first reader—we protect the body and mind from that which it cannot stand. And so, perhaps, in our readings (and writings) we wrap the texts about our bodies for protection. Or we enter the text's covers as a child might secrete herself in the closet and peer out onto the world to survey the territory through the slit in the door left slightly ajar. But we must be cautious to remember that it is a subjective view of the world we create from our own limited perspectives. In our readings, we see through the glass darkly. Of her own novel, *Oranges are Not the Only Fruit,* Winterson (2011, 6) says, "I wrote a story I could live with. The other was too painful. I could not survive it." So, too, I think, with all our reading: we read the stories we can live with. Winterson and Auster acknowledge that our bodies remember though we (the eponymous "we") do not always consciously identify what it is that our bodies remember. But in the texts we read and write we transform our emotions into feelings; we imagine, and when we read well we do not presume that our imaginings are rigorous transcription. The books I read and write are partial truths that I read partially. The truth evades me always. I believe, as did Tolstoy, "in the inexorable power of the present moment: in our inability to do away with the sum of conditions which cumulatively determine our basic categories, an order which we can never fully describe or, otherwise than by some immediate awareness of it, come to know" (Berlin, 2000, 495). Reading and writing stretches me to the limits of my consciousness.

So, we read the novels we can live with; the others are too painful and we could not survive them. In our writing and our reading, we seek strategies to keep on keeping on. Our emotions become feelings when they are understood in context—then they can be written and even read—but they are not the whole story. Milosz writes in his autobiography: "The passing over of certain periods important for oneself, but requiring an explanation, will be a token of respect for those undergrounds that exist in all of us and that are better left in peace." I read the story I can live with; the other I could not survive; my friend Reuven reads the same book but it is different. Thus, every book has its Other, and that Other book, too, may be touched to touch the man. Roth (1988, 172) says, "With autobiography there's always another text, a countertext, if you will, to the one presented." Stories, Winterson (2011) writes, are compensatory: since we cannot say too many things because they are so painful "we write what we do to compensate for what can't be said. Writing breaks the silence by maintaining it." "Whenever I feel afraid, . . . I whistle a happy tune," Anna sings in *The King and I*. And memoirist Patricia Hampl (1999, 28) writes, "We all have our ways of whistling in the dark." As for me, I choose another book from the shelf. What have I lost and what will I find?

Books send me out from my native land to the land that they might show me. Thus, my reading is always autobiographical. I choose my reading by the question my life presents to me about my existence, and from my reading I seek some response. There is a story by Nobel Laureate Shmuel Yosef Agnon (1995), entitled "The Book That Was Lost." It is the story of a young European Jewish scholar who by chance comes upon the unbound manuscript of Rabbi Shmaria, the Dayan. Shmaria was a great scholar of the code of Jewish law called the Shulkhan Aruch, produced by Joseph Caro in the sixteenth century. Caro's code intended to give a simple statement of the law as it affected the life of the ordinary Sephardic Jew; "shulkhan aruch" means "the prepared table." Earlier codes had developed over the long history of the Jewish people, but they were often in conflict with the differing conditions in which Jews lived in the Diaspora; different communities followed different rulings and interpretations depending upon their particular circumstances. The genius of Caro's work is that it ignored all areas of law no longer applicable to the life in the sixteenth century and omitted all references to earlier codes. The Shulkhan Aruch purports to be definitive though it is, finally, parochial. That is, Caro tended to rely on the Spanish authorities who held sway in the society in which Caro lived and worked, and he gave insufficient attention to the needs of Polish (Ashkenaz) Jews whose history and lives developed and necessitated differing practices. Nevertheless, and despite its shortcomings, the Shulkhan Aruch was the last comprehensive law code produced, perhaps because it appeared at the advent of the printing press and many more copies of it appeared than could have been possible for any of the earlier codes.

Now, Rabbi Shmaria was especially interested in a particular section of Caro's code called Orah Hayyim, "The Way of Life," that dealt with the practices of daily life—a section the narrator notes (ironically, I suspect) about which most commentators remained unconcerned. After all, what else would a serious scholar be less interested in than the laws concerning the prosaic practices of daily life! One of Shmaria's favorite glosses on this neglected section was the commentary of Magen Avraham, one of the few scholars who had dealt with this section of the code. But because Magen Avraham had been so poor, he could not readily purchase proper materials on which to write. When he wrote, he would use whatever surface was available on which to collect his thoughts; indeed, much of his commentary was written on the walls and furniture of his meager home. But when a bit of money would come into his hands, he would "purchase a small piece of paper, compose his thoughts, and jot down their essence in extremely concise language." Circumstances inclined Magen Avraham's work to extreme succinctness and concision. His work was very obscure.

Rabbi Shmaria, nonetheless, was enamored of the commentary of Magen Avraham on Orah Hayyim, and Shmaria devoted twelve years of his own life to the explication of each and every word, phrase, and expression in Magen Avraham's commentary. As do many of us when we study, Shmaria took notes and wrote his own thoughts and reflections on the subject of Magen Avraham's work. When Shmaria was finished, he collected his own manuscript pages and invited a bookbinder to his home to discuss the preparation of his manuscript into book form for publication. The bookbinder arrived carrying the pages of another unbound manuscript. He casually put these pages down while he professionally examined Shmaria's work. But because Shmaria was an ardent scholar, while the bookbinder studied Shmaria's own manuscript the Rabbi leafed casually through the pages of the manuscript that the binder had carried in with him. "What," Shmaria asked the bookbinder, "is the subject of these pages you have carried in with you?" The bookbinder answered that the pages contained the commentary of another scholar on the exact matter that Rabbi Shmaria had labored so long in his scholarship—the work of Magen Avraham. Sighing deeply, Shmaria said "I have been preceded by another; there is no need of my work" (Agnon, 1995, 129). And he dismissed the bookbinder and put his unbound pages away. (Shmaria's humility, I think, is not the common practice in today's scholarly circles.)

Many years passed. One day the young scholar in our story discovers in the attic of the Great Synagogue in his town the very unbound pages of the manuscript of Shmaria's commentary on Magen Avraham's commentary. Showing the work to various scholars in his community, our protagonist is assured that there are several interesting interpretations in Shmaria's work and that, indeed, they deserve a public viewing. The scholar learns that a new library is being organized in Jerusalem and the administrators are seeking contributions from all over the Diaspora. Poor himself, the scholar sacrifices what little monies he has to send the manuscript copy of Shmaria's work on Magen Avraham as a donation to the library in Jerusalem.

Finally, the scholar himself settles in Jerusalem and goes to the famous library to which he had sent the book. But upon arriving there he discovers that the book cannot be found. No record of it could be discovered. "Many times did I go to the library and many times did I speak to the librarian. When I didn't mention Rabbi Shmaria's book, the librarian would, and he would say, 'I still haven't found it, but if not today, then tomorrow.' So the years passed. That librarian went the way of all flesh and the librarian who succeeded him also passed on, but the book was not found. What a pity," the scholar lamented, "the book was lost" (135). I think that the book that changed my life is the book that was lost. I am certain that this book is a modest commentary on the complex codes (themselves, as 1 have said, already a commentary on previous codes) that bound my life; this, alas, lost book would afford me precious insights into the complexities and questions that beset my daily existence. I read regularly to find this book.

In order to exist, societies must, of necessity, produce norms of thought and behavior that facilitate some form of communal living. These productions, or codes, might also be understood as commentaries on the forms of living given authority by a specific social order. The common history that a society authorizes as its narrative is the efflux of a set of behavioral codes (and its commentaries) that are given priority in the composition of the history. The written codes and commentaries that a society produces define the social compact to which it aspires. These codes and commentaries engender their own commentaries. We all,

I think, choose to live according to a variety of explicit and implicit codes. These codes and commentaries regulate our behavior and thought even as they influence our thought and behavior. These codes and commentaries facilitate entrance into and movement within particular societies of our choosing. Discovering the myriad codes that function in the societies in which I function involves constant attention. The study of these codes inspires analysis and annotation, or commentaries. The codes themselves, like the Shulkhan Aruch, are writ large and acquire authority. And though they purport to be absolute, they are themselves only commentary; they require continuous interpretation and comment. They demand gloss; they spawn further commentary.

Sometimes codes remain unwritten or incompletely recorded: assimilation is, after all, the almost always unsuccessful attempt to adopt the complete code of a desired society; and assimilation almost always fails precisely because the whole code is never expressed and because it is a code that only partially reveals entrance into a particular society. These codes, only partially revealed though they be, nonetheless are authoritative and provoke commentary. Several codes are elaborately, even eloquently, written; they are made quite public. There is in my social world an extraordinarily wide variety of published exemplars of codes that attempt to define and order life: the Declaration of Independence, the Constitution, the Ten Commandments, Brown vs. the Board of Education, Emily Post's etiquette, national curriculums and standards. They mean to define order. I suspect that each culture (and a society is composed of many cultures) produces a variety of shulkhan aruchs that offer structures for the exercise of life. Nonetheless, they are all codes that establish the practices of daily life. The larger issues that the codes address and upon which they are based, such as what kind of society do we mean to produce and what kind of people do we mean to be, are often relatively obvious. Perhaps that is why they are so hotly and publically contested. The more mundane issues do not so soon become the subject of public discourse: where is the code that determines the bedtimes routines that ought to function in my household? Where are the rules to establish on which nights to require baths, or how large a "no, thank you" portion must be to be counted as such? Nonetheless, I want immediately to find some commentary to help me on my muddled way. Much commentary, I think, must be written about these practices, though often the code on which it is a comment remains unspoken. Of course, all behavioral norms rise up from some ideal base that is assumed but not voiced. Or if it is voiced, it is insufferably vague: "Well, I want you to be good children. And good grownups. And free and productive citizens. And critical thinkers." "I don't get it," they say. My children are taught a great deal by the codes and commentaries by which I live and that I speak. My therapist and my Rabbi listen *ad infinitum* and *ad nauseam* to my commentary on these codes. I read to observe and to discover and to apprehend the codes and their commentaries. The book that is lost will clear things up considerably.

There are in my social world illimitable books that serve as exegesis—commentary—on those codes that are themselves commentary. I have even, alas, written a few myself. All books (oh, and art and music and sculpture and all such production—but I am concerned primarily here with the written word) are in some way a response to and an explication of those explicit and implicit codes. Even the world of which we dream must derive from the world in which we live; what else is Utopia but a codification of ideals? I must know that the sparrow can fall if I am ever to see it fall. This lost book that has changed my life has addressed the daily lives I have lived and will continue to live; this lost book is a commentary on the code (that is itself a commentary) and will offer me inestimable insight into the realization of my dreams. There are, alas and thankfully, no end to the commentaries concerning the code; while I search for the book that was lost, I bide my time with those that are found. The work of one is always preceded by another. The book that is lost is original but not new. As Winterson reminds me, someone has been there before! But that book has some interesting commentary that deserves to be read.

Somewhere out there is the book that is lost, which if I would read would settle some of my most pressing dilemmas. Somewhere out there is the book that was lost, which if I could find would elaborate some of the more obscure commentary on the significant codes in my life and provide me, perhaps, with answers for some of the more difficult questions my living has raised. Somewhere out there in the vast library of the world rests the book that was lost awaiting my reading! I have consecrated my life to looking for that lost book; I prowl bookstores and secondhand bookstores and libraries and other people's basements. Believing in print, I have committed my life to the efficacy of the written word and I search for exactly that book which would comment transformatively on my existence. The book that changes my life is the book that was lost—the book for which I continue to search.

It will, I am sure, alter my life. And, alas, if it is not found today, it will certainly be retrieved tomorrow. Perhaps Godot carries it even now!

Summer evenings in Wisconsin can be exquisite. For some reason, which I should probably have learned in high school, sunset occurs very late in this northerly longitude; it might be 10:00 p.m. before all traces of sunlight (except perhaps in the moon's glow) are gone. It is tempting during Wisconsin summers to forget the hour. But children live here, and despite the light it must be time for bed. Now, in our home reading has always been a bedtime ritual accompanied by many practices particular to the occupants of this household. When the children were very young, we read to them assiduously in the evening at bedtime. One, two, seven books. Emma and Anna Rose would choose several books they desired, and I would choose one or two in which I had some personal or pedagogical interest. We would lie together on their beds with only the reading light lit and we would share the books. Like everything else, there were good and not so good nights, nights when in the reading we established a complex bond between the process and the books and the participants, and nights when we read separate and alone. And yet we persisted. As Emma and Anna Rose learned the formal aspects of attachment to print, I began to listen to them read the wonderfully exciting books (their term) they brought from school and the numerous Beginning-to-Read series that their neurotic father purchased in the anticipation of their emerging facility and his desperate desire that they become readers.

I loved reading with my daughters—I love reading. Intellectually I know that there are other ways to learn and other expressions of intelligences, but emotionally I remain committed to print and the printed word. And when they became independent readers and no longer required (or desired!) that I read to them, it became again possible to return to my own cherished nightly reading. And since it was always my intention to read in the evening anyway, it did not make too much difference *where* it was that I would sit and read. Thus, it became custom that we continue our bedtime reading together as independent readers: Emma and Anna Rose would read their books and I would read mine. We even purchased a comfy chair for their rooms and for the adult member of the reading community. In any week, each would finish two or three books every week. We are not so rapid, but then, there is another child who yet requires our services as reader.

The summer sky tonight reminds me of the colors of a Monet painting. I sit tonight with Anna Rose. We are reading, as I have said.

"Dad," she says, "can I ask you a question?"

"Sure."

"What's your favorite book?"

This is a typical question. I think she is testing her own standards. Whatever book I name she will require its plot and demand its significance. She will use my response to contemplate upon the book that she presently reads.

"Oh, darling," I respond, "I've read so many books that I don't think I can choose one book to be my favorite."

Anna Rose is a clever child (but what else would her teacher–educator father say about his child?). When she cannot get a direct answer, she pursues a diversionary tack.

"Okay, then, what book are you writing now?" she persists.

A clever ploy, I think. What better way to enchant me into revealing the secret than to flatter me by inquiring about my own work?

"Actually," I tell her, "I'm writing an article about the book that changed my life."

She contemplates this topic briefly. She lifts her glass to her lips.

"Which one are you writing about?"

She takes a drink of water.

"That's a great question. I suppose I'm writing about all of them. Every book I read changes me because once I finish reading the book I can't remember who I was before I had read it. I think that that is what reading is in large part—the use of something already in existence to create something that doesn't yet exist. But the new can no longer remember the old without influencing the memory by the very fact of its newness."

"I don't get it."

"Well, let's see, Anna Rose, if I can explain. Look, what was the last book you read?"

"*Pride and Prejudice.*"

"Okay, now, when you started that book you were Anna Rose Peck-Block who had never read *Pride and Prejudice*. You knew lots of things and many people. You had read lots of books. But you did not know Elizabeth Bennett or Mr. Darcy, right?"

"Yes."

"And you had never visited the world in which Elizabeth Bennett or Mr. Darcy lived and met and had personalities and had disagreements and fell in love, did you?"

"That's true."

"Okay, now that you have finished the book you have not only met the Bennett family and Mr. Darcy, but actually lived with them for a brief time. You were involved with them during the time in which you read the book. You listened to them talk, you watched them behave—you got angry or anxious or upset or pleased. Their lives mixed with your life and as a result you changed. In your meeting with them you have changed. Before you read the book you did not know them at all—indeed, you probably never saw anyone act exactly the way they did, nor have exactly the same thoughts, nor look the way you imagined them to look. If nothing else, you met some interesting characters who behaved in very particular ways. Somehow, in even the smallest way, you will be influenced by your having met them. You'll see the world through the additional lens of *Pride and Prejudice*. You won't be able to avoid it, and you may not even know it. I think that by reading that book you even changed Elizabeth and Darcy—but because they are characters in a book they don't know it."

"Huh?"

"Well, no one exactly like you has ever read *Pride and Prejudice* before, and so no one has ever seen these characters and their lives through your eyes."

"Well, that explains how I can change them, but how could they change me?"

"Try this. Can you remember who you were before you read that book? Can you remember exactly who you were before you read *Pride and Prejudice*?"

"No, of course not."

"Then you must have changed. Of course, at the same time you were reading the book you were involved in a very active life and you were changing daily—all of the change cannot be ascribed to your reading of the book. But your engagement in *Pride and Prejudice* changed you, and I don't think you can exactly remember who you were before you read the book. Every book changes us in ways we can hardly define. For example, I can't remember who I was before I read, say, *Walden*."

Thoreau writes: "It is not all books that are as dull as their readers. There are probably words addressed to our condition exactly, which, if we could really hear and understand, would be more salutary than the morning or the spring to our lives, and possibly put a new aspect on the face of things for us. How many a man has dated a new era in his life from the reading of a book?" I am comforted that the quality of my reading rests within my purview and that the sense of every book is of my devise. Thoreau reminds me that it is not the book I read that is important so much as it is I, the reader, who establishes the significance of the book. Were we to ask the right questions, any book might be the one that renews our lives.

Spring and morning are not incidental to Thoreau's world view. In *Walden*, he crows that that day dawns only to which we are awake; he marvels that spring bodes the thawing of Walden Pond—what once was dead comes alive again. Yet, in the lines quoted above, Thoreau would ascribe to reading a power greater than that of either spring or morning. Reading for Thoreau is no small event. Rather, I think that reading incorporates morning and spring within; we need not await any season nor time of day but produce our own renascence in reading the book—indeed, reading any book. Perhaps it is that in our perspectives in reading we create mornings and springs for ourselves, and with every book possess the opportunity to renew our lives. The book that changes my life is the one to which I am awake. It is not the book that awakens me but I who awaken the book. The book that changes me is the book I have changed.

"What do you think you want to read next?" I ask my children. It is a cautious question. I do not want to direct the reading but I do mean to further the process. It is a precarious position I occupy: my recommendations are suspect though my intent sincere. Oscar Wilde (in Manguel, 1996, 313) has written: "To tell people what to read is as a rule either useless or harmful, for the true appreciation of literature is a question of temperament not of teaching, to Parnassus there is no primer, and nothing that one can learn is ever worth learning. But to tell people what not to read is a very different matter, and I recommend it as a mission to the University Extension scheme." Of course, with my children I too often tell them what I think they should be reading; there are things I feel they must learn—codes and commentaries they must read. But it pleases me (usually) when Emma and Anna Rose now refuse my recommendation and choose their own reading; they have their desires. I wonder who they will be when they finish the book. And the book that changes my life is the book that changes theirs.

Of course, Wilde's dictum places a huge crimp in my course syllabi. Unless under the heading "Required Texts" I assign "the book that was lost."

"And which book would that be, Professor Block? If it was lost, where can I find it?"

"Exactly," I would respond.

CHAPTER 3

ON THE ASKING OF QUESTIONS

"Dr. Block, can I ask you a question?" she said.

I HAD JUST LEFT A CLASS THAT I HELD TO HAVE BEEN AN UTTER FAILURE, and I was walking disconsolately back to my office carrying my books and papers. I felt as I supposed the tragic Sisyphus might have as he pushed that rock up the hill: engaged in a useless and frustratingly endless task. In this particular class we had been discussing John Updike's *The Centaur*, a novel I have over the years adored, and one I considered an appropriate final text from which to read in a Foundations of Education class occupied by first- and second-year students who were studying to become teachers.

The Centaur is the story of a teacher, a very good teacher, I think, but one sorely troubled by the nature of his profession, as perhaps are all very good teachers. That is, George Caldwell suffers from too many questions, the greatest of all that stems from the doubt he experiences concerning the meaning of his work. "I wouldn't mind plugging ahead at something I wasn't any good at," Caldwell laments, "if I knew what the hell the point of it all was. I ask and nobody'll tell me" (Updike, 1963, 102). Despite his doubt, George is hardly a failure; indeed, the only person in the book who doesn't think highly of him *as a teacher* is himself, but George struggles with knowledge, tormented and seemingly frustrated by it, not unlike Sisyphus who was tortured by his rock. "Ignorance is bliss," Caldwell announces to his colleague Phillips. "That's the lesson I've gotten out of life" Like Chiron, his mythological counterpart, Caldwell had meant to bring the children out of darkness, but to him all of his knowledge seems to point only to darkness and to death. Indeed, whatever knowledge he seems to possess seems inadequate and ineffective. He appears at an appointment to have his tooth extracted by a dentist who once had been his student. As the dentist works unskillfully, Caldwell considers that "the pain branching in his head [w]as a consequence of some failing in his own teaching, a failure somewhere to inculcate in this struggling soul consideration and patience . . ." (164). George's failure seems to him to be more than intellectual; it is existential. In twentieth-century Olinger, Pennsylvania—certainly no Golden Age—the darkness seems to Caldwell pervasive and unending.

As I walked from my own classroom, I understood a little his despair.

If it is knowledge that the teacher is to communicate, Caldwell has little faith in what he offers. To his distressed student, Judith Lengel, who almost in tears bemoans, "I get so sort of sick and dizzy just trying to keep it all straight," Caldwell acknowledges regretfully, "Knowledge is a sickening thing." And when his wife, Cassie, says to him, "It must be terrible to know so much," Caldwell groans, "It is." Caldwell despairs not simply in what he knows but also in what he does not and will never know. He is a teacher with no faith either in what he does or what he is supposed to do. Suffering from severe stomach pain, George suspects cancer: "The kids have put their poison in me," he says. But Doc Appleton discovers no disease and diagnoses George's physical complaints as resulting from his existential questing: Appleton says, "You aren't a teacher, you're a learner," and asserts that this produces tension that leads to Caldwell's gastrointestinal complaint. And George has a few questions.

In his questions Caldwell (1963) asks for more than answers: this teacher searches for his life. Interestingly, his questions defy answers, and that is perhaps George's dilemma: the important questions he asks all have no answer, and yet he continues to ask them. At the school basketball game he approaches the Reverend March. "The fact is I'm sorely troubled in my mind," he announces. When March the Lutheran clergyman cavalierly inquires what troubles George, the teacher answers, "Everything. The works. I can't make it add up . . ." George searches desperately for meaning. He continues: "My old man was a Presbyterian," he explains, "and as I understand it from him there are the elect and the non-elect, the ones that have it and the ones that don't, and the ones that don't have it are never going to get it. What I could never ram through my thick skull was why the ones that don't have it were created in the first place . . ." (189). Of what value is knowledge if all it leads to is death and damnation? Why teach at all?

For me, George Caldwell represented an honest portrait of a teacher, filled as he might be with contradiction, doubt, and conflict, struggling to make relevant what often might not be, and to make sense of what often does not contextually do so. It was Caldwell's dilemmas that I had wanted the students to consider. During the semester I had offered a discussion portraying the difficulties of the teaching profession, and how very hard it was to be a teacher. Understandably and romantically, my students' concept of the classroom consisted mostly of idyllic images not unlike Chiron's mythic classroom where nothing that occurred was amiss, where the noble, well-mannered students remained eager and attentive, and where learning occurred seemingly seamlessly with little effort or without visible resistance. In my class and to this end, besides studying the ideas concerning education of several influential American educators (John Dewey, Franklin Bobbitt, Jane Addams, George Counts, Robert Hutchins, even myself!)

I had offered several case studies of student-teachers who had struggled mightily in the classroom in their attempts to become teachers (Britzman, 2003). Indeed, one of the two student-teachers chose eventually not to enter the profession after a particularly difficult and unrewarding experience in the classroom. We had studied an essay in my own text, *Ethics and Teaching* (2009), entitled "Why Should I Be a Teacher?" that called into question the intimately held myths about the profession, and a piece by David Labaree (2010), "Targeting Teachers," which spoke of the impossible nature of the teaching profession and the courageous work of those who entered into it and bore the brunt of attack and ridicule.

I wanted these essays to dispel the traditional traditions that surround teaching and that often lead many students to desire to enter it, and lead too many to disappointingly leave it. The essays portray instead the difficulties immanent in the teaching profession, and reflect upon the mostly minimal material and emotional rewards available to the practicing teacher. My students had been certain that the classroom would be an ideal place where clean, mannerly students would sit excitedly attending to whatever the teacher—in this case themselves—presented as lessons: *their* students would be absorptive sponges for the teacher's illimitable gushings. *Their* students would complete them. But the essays suggested the opposite to be true: that teachers must be brave *because* the work is so exhaustingly difficult and that the rewards would remain sometimes intangible, often rare, and always uncertain. In Updike's novel, *The Centaur,* George's success remains finally and wholly outside his comprehension, even his awareness.

My students had engaged during the semester in vigorous and (I had thought) probing, even disturbing discussions concerning the assigned essays and book chapters exploring issues central to a study of the foundations of education: philosophy, history, politics, etc., and so, I expected (or was it just hope?) that by this time in the semester, everyone would be familiar, ready, *and prepared* to engage in some heated intellectual discussion of *The Centaur*.

I was never so wrong in my life. In this particular class I was confronted by deep wells of silence. All I could hear in that classroom was the echo of my own voice as I called down into a dark cavernous abyss. I felt not unlike the student-teachers described in the two book chapters I had first assigned: confused, lost, frustrated, and upset. But unlike these novice student-teachers, I had been teaching for forty-three years! I also experienced anger and discouragement. In my questions I had probed for some stimulus to conversation but I continued to be met only by the silence. I said aloud (irrationally, because I knew no response would be forthcoming), "What is wrong with my questions? Why won't you respond? What questions would you prefer?" In silence they stared beyond me.

When I have thought about Sisyphus it is always upon the futility and meaninglessness of his task on which I have tended to focus, but today I considered that perhaps it was his misstep that had weakened his mastery over the rock and that had led to its inevitable cascade back down the mountain. He would then have to descend to begin again tomorrow the task of futilely pushing the stone back up the mountain. In myth it is sometimes said that Zeus had enchanted the boulder to roll away from Sisyphus, but today I considered that it was Sisyphus' faltering that had led to the rock's descent. After all, it was his pride that had condemned Sisyphus in the first place to this endless and ultimately meaningless task. I felt that I, too, had somewhere stumbled, and I watched helplessly as the rock rolled back down the mountain. And I despaired that the next day I would have to re-enter that classroom and begin the struggle again. I considered that in my inattentiveness I had somehow slipped on something in the classroom and that it had gotten away from me. Along with Caldwell I thought, "I wouldn't mind plugging ahead at something I wasn't any good at if I knew what the hell the point of it all was. I ask and nobody'll tell me." (Updike, 1963, 102).

When I departed class and walked back toward my office, I considered that class today had been a meaningless endeavor, and that the time devoted by all of us to the experience had been misspent. I considered that the assignment to read the book might have been for naught. I experienced serious doubts. As I contemplated what I believed had occurred in that classroom, all I could acknowledge was . . . well, that nothing had happened. "Let's go," I had said, but nobody had moved.

And then Hannah had snuck up behind me and said tentatively, "Dr. Block, can I ask you a question?" Hannah was a student in the class from which I had just fled. "Sure," I responded, ("Please," I thought, "give me some insight into what I had done wrong in that class. By your question please help me be a better teacher!") Hugging her books to her chest she asked, "Have you ever read *The Sun Also Rises*?"

This was not exactly the question that I had expected and certainly not the one I wanted, but, I considered, at least it was a question! I said, "Yes, I've read Hemingway's novel." (Ever the teacher, I felt compelled to identify the author.) And I continued, "Why do you ask, Hannah?" She looked ahead, waited a second or three, and then wondered aloud to me, "What's the point?"

I considered: this was an interesting question, and I realized that depending on how I ascribed a certain emphasis to the words, I could interpret it in at least one of two ways. First, Hannah could be asking what was the point of reading the book at all! This emphasis called into question the very nature of the life I had chosen, and I was not prepared to engage in that discussion at this time and place. Indeed, the philosophical implications of that question were so enormous for me that I feared venturing even the smallest step into this terrain without the companionship of some valued colleagues, my therapist, or a bottle of single-malt scotch. And I certainly wasn't ready to explain my life to either Hannah or myself in front of the Student Union Building on a bitterly cold winter's day in West Central Wisconsin. And so I decided not to deal with the implications of that particular emphasis to her question. I asked Hannah for further clarification. "What do you mean, Hannah, what is the point?" "Well," she said, "What is the point of the book?"

Ah, I reflected, I know where I am. Hannah wanted to know what was the *meaning* of the book; what was the book's *theme*? I have been there before. This *discovery* of *the point* was one major goal of the traditional English classroom: to read a work of literature and determine what it meant. What was the point of the book? And since it was a cold winter's day, if I could offer Hannah my response in, say, a single sentence or brief paragraph, I think she would have been very appreciative. After all, *points* are those places to which we head: arriving at some point justifies the effort, or at least completes it. Without the point, too many may hold, effort is meaningless. Sisyphus' effort, of course, has no point—that's the point! Dubious as to the point of *The Sun Also Rises*, Hannah was wondering if she had wasted her time reading the book. Without a point there would be no justification for her effort. Isn't that the Sisyphean dilemma? What was the point of all of that activity? Someone might inquire of her, "Why did you read that book?" and she might respond, "I don't know. I guess it was a waste of time, actually. I didn't know what the point of it was." If Hannah didn't get the point, then there was either something wrong with her or with the book; her question to me on whether the book had a point helped her avoid the possibility of her own potential intellectual failings.

But wasn't I having the same problem with the class I had just left? What had been the point of all that silence? Hadn't we all wasted our time?

I considered that Hannah's was a pedagogical problem; Hannah had learned to read *that* way—*to get the point*—in school. Many years ago I wrote a book (1994) concerning this very pedagogical issue. It didn't sell well. But Hannah learned to read in this manner in large part because in schools teachers ask all of the questions; it is they who supposedly possess all of the answers and know the point to which these Socratic questions must lead. Teachers offer praise to students for the correct answer and voice disapproval (mild and severe) to students for wrong ones. However it may be finally defined, the Socratic method of education requires the teacher to ask questions that call into question the reasoning of the students in order to lead that student to (a) an appreciation of his own ignorance; or (b) an acceptance of the answer, of the truth to which the teacher would lead the student. In either case, the Socratic method is an educationally accepted avenue for the development of critical thinking in students: to examine rationally the foundations of one's ideas and understand and evaluate the power of them. Thus, though it might be true that Socrates confessed his ignorance, his questions were actually grounded in knowledge and an awareness of the direction to which he was philosophically leading his student: Socrates was very aware that his questions would direct his student toward the point.

But there are alternatives to this way of knowing and this pedagogical model: there is another view of knowledge that eschews this particular pedagogy of critical thinking. Giambattista Vico, in *On the Study of Methods of Our Time* (1990, 34), asserts that "It is therefore impossible to assess human affairs by the inflexible standard of abstract right; we must rather gauge them by the pliant Lesbic rule, which does not conform bodies to itself, but adjusts itself to their contours." This Lesbic rule refers to things that cannot be determined by law. Given the exigencies and contingencies intrinsic to actual living, the rationalist Socratic method of questioning to reach the foundational point of anything concerning human affairs, much less of truth, is impossible.

Isaiah Berlin (2013) explores such a view in "Vico's Concept of Knowledge." Berlin argues after Vico that the Cartesian insistence on deductive methods as the sole path to knowledge is wrong: "It is," Berlin argues, "a kind of pedagogic despotism which suppresses various other faculties and methods of mental development, especially, the imagination" (142). Alternatively, Berlin argues, Vico "uncovers" (Berlin's term, 147) a form of knowing that derives from the imagination. Vico argues that it is wrong to say that we can *only* know what we have made, an argument whence derives the Cartesian hegemony of geometry and science as the quintessential source of knowledge. Reading and its pedagogies—indeed, educational practice itself—have become more and more organized by scientifically validated research that defines what occurs during education and how it might be more perfectly measured. Best practices must conform to the rigor and exactitude of scientific validation. As there is truth, it must be measureable and the authorities demand, it will be measured!

Rather, Vico argues, there is a knowledge that derives from the imagination and it has no measure. Vico "uncovered a sense of knowing which is basic to all humane studies: the sense in which I know what it is to be poor, to fight for a cause, to belong to a nation, to join or abandon a Church or a party, to feel nostalgia, terror, the omnipresence of a god, to understand a gesture, a work of art, a joke, a man's character, that one is transformed or lying to oneself" (147). This form of phenomenological knowing occurs because humans have the capacity "to reconstruct imaginatively . . . what they did and what they suffered, for what they hoped, wished and feared, what efforts were made and what works in which they engaged" (147). This form of knowing, Vico argues, is not analyzable except in terms of itself, nor can it be identified by measurement or objective examination. It is not a form of knowing that may be discovered or even measured by science. Rather, this awareness can be known by examples.

One can, for example, learn to be a teacher through an imaginative identification with George Caldwell, the teacher, and equally as well, if not better than, from the instrumentalist pedagogy of best practices and instructional methods so ubiquitous in teacher education programs. Hence, it is here that I recognize the importance of literature and the necessity for a certain pedagogy of reading. Vico writes,

The poet teaches by delighting what the philosopher teaches austerely. Both teach moral duties; both depict human habits and behavior; both incite to virtue and deter from vice. But the philosopher, addressing himself to cultivated men, treats these matters in a generic way. The poet, instead, because his business is with the majority of men, induces persuasion by giving plastic portrayals of exalted actions and characters; he works, as it were, with 'invented' examples. As a result, he may depart from the daily semblances of truth, in order to be able to frame a loftier semblance of reality. He departs from inconstant, unpredictable nature in order to pursue a more constant, more abiding reality. He creates imaginary figments which, in a way, are more real than physical reality itself.

Vico suggests that we might learn to focus not on the answer but on the person who answers.

Teachers might "uncover" a form of knowing that derives from the imagination and the activity of imagining. "Imagining," says Kendall Walton (1990, 22), "is a way of toying with, exploring, trying out new and far-fetched ideas," and there are no constraints upon this power except those of our unconscious and the accidental circumstances of our lives. In Walton's terms, works of fiction are props in the game of make-believe—in imagining—and we may read even biographies or histories as we do novels if we undertake *to imagine*—to play with—whatever propositions a book expresses. From this perspective, "Works become analyzable not by whether they are correct or incorrect, skillful or inept, a success or a failure, but whether they are profound or shallow, realistic or unrealistic, perceptive or stupid, alive or dead" (Berlin, 2013, 148). These judgments are available to the imagination, and I believe they begin not with the question, "What is the point?" but rather with, "What do I imagine?" Albeit a novel, *The Centaur* might give students an imaginative insight into an unidealized teacher. They might know his doubt, his frustration, his questing, his struggle, because they have had experience *as human beings* with intensities of these feelings. They have lived in the community of others in and out of school who have felt such emotions, and because they might *imagine*—play with—what George might be feeling. Berlin (147) teaches me that even if the student might be wrong or his knowledge invalid, that he may be lying or deluding himself or misidentifying his experience, nonetheless, that student *knows* something in a way that is quite different than knowing that "this tree is taller than that, or that Caesar was assassinated on the Ides of March, or that seventeen is a prime number, or that 'vermilion' cannot be defined, or that the king in chess can only move one square at a time." It had been my desire that students *know* what it might feel like to be a teacher, and that was my motive for assigning Updike's novel, *The Centaur*. But I had asked all of the wrong questions!

For Hannah and her comrades, the emphasis on arriving at *the* point—abstract truth—has led to the ubiquity of standardized and multiple choice tests that are forever asking what is the main idea of a selection and for which only one answer is acceptable. "Which sentence best expresses the main idea of the passage?" "Why do you think Huck Finn lies to the slave traders to save Jim?" There is a critical method that teachers have passed along to students by the questions they asked and the answers that they accepted. Students are taught that when they read, say, imaginative fiction, they must seek out the *hidden* meaning of texts. The questions teachers ask are meant to lead students to the concealed trove that holds an author's intentions. "Read between the lines" students are counseled, though it has long been clear to me that if a student reads between the lines they will come across only white space: they will miss the book. Textbooks are to be treated as holy writ, absorbed absolutely and trusted as revelation. Students are asked to answer questions and not to ask them!

Reading is seldom considered an open activity engaged in for its own sake; students are rarely taught how to *know* a meaning of the texts they are assigned to read from the lives that they are living. Students are rarely asked whether the works they read are "profound or shallow, realistic or unrealistic, perceptive or stupid, alive or dead." Students are not often taught how to interrogate the worlds of the texts they are assigned; to wonder: "Into what worlds does the book invite me? Might I want to enter that world? Are these people about whom I read those about whom I am curious? Are these people I would be interested in knowing?" And for each of these questions, the autobiographical inquiry ought to be *why, or why not?*

Rather, reading is performed in order to "get the point" so that some question posed by some authority might be correctly answered. Vico (1990, 34) says: "Satisfied with abstract truth alone, and not being gifted with common sense, unused to following probability, those doctrinaires do not bother to find out whether their opinion is held by the generality and whether the things that are truths to them are also such to other people." The question students most ask of teachers in school is, "Teacher, will this be on the test?" It was the unforthcoming answer to this problem that had led Caldwell's student, Judy Lengel, to tears. The questions most asked of students in school is, "What is the meaning of the passage?" The answer is often silence. *Mea culpa.* I have defined my class.

And so I considered that Hannah's question suggested for her a limited repertoire of questions. She was expressing the only legitimate question that she had been taught (perhaps even permitted) to ask: one that would lead to a definitive answer concerning, in this case, the novel's point. I considered that Hannah had presented me with an essential pedagogical problem: have we organized education so that students only proffer answers rather than ask questions? Were my questions only a pedagogy of answers? Perhaps the questions I had posed in the classroom had been merely ploys with which I would disguise my ultimate purpose: to arrive at the point. I felt hoisted on my own petard! And I wondered, what did *I* still want to know about the novel that

I might learn from my students' reading of it, and could I actually go into the class with questions rather than answers? How might the questions help me give up the pedagogical stance and engage in real pedagogy?

I think that this is far more than a pedagogical problem: in Hannah's question, I think I am confronted with a social issue of some consequence. Hannah's question suggested to me that she has learned that she should be focused on ends and not means. This is a paradox because if I mean to create life-long learners, a statement inherent in *every* mission statement of *every* educational institution of which I am aware, then Hannah should be learning about means and not ends. But "What's the point?" is a question about ends and not about means. I thought back to Phaedrus, in Robert Pirsig's *Zen and the Art of Motorcycle Maintenance* (2006): there he says that the top of the mountain defines the sides, but it is on the sides of the mountain that life grows. Hannah's question concerned the point—the peak—and was blind to the sides. I was thinking, too, about Socrates, whose method is yet held up as the perfect model of the classroom. But Socrates always knew the final conclusion to which his questions would lead: it was the cleverness of his artifice and the philosophical questions that were raised that have long intrigued scholars and pedagogues.

I paused a moment to breathe and said, "Hannah, perhaps the book doesn't have a point." I tried to make a joke: "If books had points, then they would hurt people."

Hannah didn't laugh.

I continued: "But perhaps you might ask a different question."

"Like what?" she asked.

"Well, what kind of world does the book portray? Would you want to live in the world of *The Sun Also Rises*?" I said. "Well, that's really two questions, but they are related."

Beginning with the second question first, Hannah said, "No, I wouldn't."

"Well, why not?" I asked.

"All they do is drink, and screw around, and criticize each other?" she answered.

"Well, why do they do these things?"

Her face wrinkled a bit. "Well, I don't know," she offered.

Hannah's is a standard response. I tell students that it is not true that they do not know, but it is certainly the case that they don't trust what they do know, or that they do not know that what is running through their mind is what knowing is about. A question is, I remembered, the beginning of knowledge. "Well, what do you think?" I insisted. And for just a few precious minutes, as we walked down the block on a bitter-cold winter's day, Hannah and I discussed Hemingway's novel. I like to think (because I am a teacher) Hannah learned a few things about *The Sun Also Rises* and maybe even about asking questions. I learned that the failure of the class hadn't been all my fault and yet had been very much the rock on which I had stumbled. And I think I learned a bit about a new set of questions I might ask the next time I teach *The Centaur*.

Our students are taught to seek answers or, even worse, they learn to seek *the* answer, but they haven't the foggiest idea how to ask questions other than "When is the paper due?" "Will that be on the test?" and "What grade am I getting in this class?" After all, almost all of their worth as students has been derived from bubbling in answers to questions on standardized short answer tests. Much of the time they are the targets for answers to questions they have not asked. I suspect they do not even know that they are authorized to ask questions. In schools, at least, the question is merely the route to an answer, and if they do not have a ready answer, then they revert to silence and await the next question. Or if the answer is too ready, then they do not want to expend their energy to give it: they will wait for the question that will allow them to show their mettle. Our students have not been yet taught to ask another question or to turn any answer to which they might arrive into another question.

There is a story about a very rich man who gives all of his wealth to a very old woman who possesses a chest filled with answers. And when the man opens the chest he discovers thousands of pieces of paper and on each one is written a sentence: "Eat breakfast," "Marry him," "If you must," "Seventy-six." And the man is very happy. "Now," the man excitedly cries, "I have the answer to all things!" But, in fact, the man has purchased nothing, for what good are the answers without the right question? Our students don't know how to ask questions because they have been taught to seek only the answers. The only question they seem to ask is "What is the point?" or some related question, such as "Why do I have to learn this?"

But I want to say as well that this is not merely a pedagogical condition: I do not intend to join the horrid chorus of critics who decry the state of our schools, our teachers, and our educational system. Rather, I think that this issue is a social one as well. We have created a society that is not interested in questions. We have come as a society to expect and to value only the answer into which we have placed all of our faith, and have reserved little respect for the unanswerable question. We have assumed an instrumentalist stand: the answer always tells us what must be done though, of course, we need not do it. Paradoxically, it is the question that inspires movement and requires that something *be* done, and it is the isolated answer that makes independent movement unnecessary. The question leads us out to we know not where—to the sea and the white whale—and the answer draws us back into the familiar to crash ultimately upon the Lee Shore.

The question implies an unknown, a sense of mystery. There is a dangerous excitement in the question. Perhaps our society has lost its pursuit of the delight of the mystery, magic, and enchantment replete in the question. Questions open the world, and answers close it down. Questions are the enemies of falseness, but the answer falsely promises fulfillment. We are told that when the genome project is complete, we will know everything there is to know about the human being, and all questions about human behavior will be finally answered. But I do not believe this at all: will the map of my genes tell me why I have fallen in love with one and not another, and what I should do about it? Will it tell me why today for breakfast I want oatmeal and not eggs? How will knowing my genetic map improve my senses of humor or compassion? The question acknowledges that there is more to know, and the answer puts an end to curiosity. The question opens the world to speculation, and the answer closes it to wonder. There is nothing beyond the answer, but by the question the world is open to possibility.

Of course, the question must be an honest one. Too many of our questions already contain the answer we desire. "Isn't this a lovely painting?" is not a question but a statement. "Why do I like this painting?" is a question that demands a response. But for the teacher the dilemma remains that if we ask questions that have no answer, then how can we begin to quantify the knowledge that students are supposed to acquire? I realized that as I had moved through the course I had not asked enough honest questions. I had demanded comprehension, but I already had in mind what must be understood. The entire first part of this chapter gives sufficient evidence of that: the disappointment I experienced is that "they" didn't get "my" point.

I like to think that Hannah and I opened the world a bit on our walk from a class that I thought had closed it. We had briefly played together with *The Sun Also Rises* and maybe gave to each other the opportunity to imagine a different world today and a different classroom tomorrow.

CHAPTER 4

Saint Joan in the Classroom

I AM BETRAYED BY THE CURRENT PUBLIC CALUMNY inflicted upon teachers in today's public schools. I am a teacher, and I take offense. It isn't even that they are talking maliciously about me behind my back, whispering in school bathroom stalls and government back corridors, but that they accuse me in public of treasonous crimes for which at best there is no evidence and at worst are mere fabrications. They speak as if I were not even present and capable of responding to their absurd charges. They ascribe to me powers I only wish I could have even as they refuse to admit to their responsibility for the conditions their actions have fostered and in which I—we—are constrained to function. Public policy and discourse has been promulgated on educational premises long disputed, on statistics long discredited by evidences to the contrary, and by programs designed not to offer assistance to public education troubled by serious financial shortages but to destroy the very foundation and fabrics of this central democratic institution.

Public rhetoric (rhetoric: the art of convincing and *not* the art of truth!) argues that a student's learning is the responsibility of the teacher, argues that the most important element in a student's success in school rests with the quality of the teacher, and that the maintenance of US power depends on the quality of the education our children receive. That quality, they say, rests exclusively with the competence of the teacher. America, they say, is in decline, and from the tenor of the public rhetoric (the art of convincing and *not* the art of truth) we are led to believe that the schools must be at present filled for the most part with incompetent practitioners—that would be me and that would be us—to whose ineptitude may be assigned the waning political and economic power of the United States. Our future as a nation is endangered by the failures of our public school system of education and the teachers and administrators who are charged with its and the nation's continuance. The opening lines of the 1983 report, *A Nation at Risk: The Imperative for Educational Reform*, still serves as the received judgment on the state of our schools: "If an unfriendly power had attempted to impose on America the mediocre educational performance that exists today, we might well have viewed it as an act of war. As it stands, we have allowed this to happen to ourselves." Having been written by politicians and bureaucrats, the report ascribes this treason to the educational institutions and to the teachers who work in them. To paraphrase Pogo, according to the politicos, the enemy is "them." For forty-two years I have been them! In the current invective aimed at the schools systems, *they* intend to fix *us*.

Current teaching initiatives, from the institution of common core standards, the pervasiveness of high-stakes testing, the recent institution of Educational Teacher Preparation Assessment (edTPA), and the development of mandatory statewide teacher assessment systems such as the Observation and Appraisal Management System (OASYS) are all premised on an assumption that the teaching profession is filled with the ineffectual and lame; that unless teachers' behaviors are precisely prescribed and monitored rigorously, that unless teachers are assigned exactly what to teach in the classrooms—often from precisely scripted manuscripts of even what to say and when it must be said—then those very same sites will remain silent and empty. We are supposed to accept that the only measure of educational effectiveness rests in *their* dubious measurable standardized outcomes, and that an ever-increasing system of policing measures is required to hold teachers to their responsibilities. These initiatives argue that how well a teacher teaches may be simply assessed on how high her students score on the tests. Value added—the idea that a teacher's effectiveness should be measured by the change in a student's test score following a term in the class—has become a common means to evaluate teachers; in Wisconsin, such measures might count as much as fifty percent of a teacher's evaluative report.

In this perspective education exists in a hermetically sealed system, the classroom a self-contained refuge from the confusion and complexity of the world that must be (but cannot be) left at the guarded school door. As if poverty, hunger, and violence are irrelevant factors in a child's educational experience so long as the teacher is competent and the material demanding enough. In this perspective all responsibility for learning rests with the teacher who *sometimes* is supplied with a spoonful of sugar to help the medicine go down, but who recently, due to severe budget cuts in educational appropriations, is often left without either the sugar or sometimes even the spoons. Learning is understood as the simple transference of cultural norms to the next generation by the activity of the teacher under the guidance of state standards and the observant watchful gazes of psychometricians and politicians. As if education was ever about consumption and not production.

And what is education about, then, if it is not the simple increase in test scores? And of what does consist the teacher's responsibility in today's classrooms. In a 1915 essay entitled "The Moral Obligation to Be Intelligent," John Erskine advanced the idea that intelligence ought to be primary among our modern virtues. I believe that schools promote—should promote—intelligence. Erskine writes, "We really seek intelligence not for the answers it may suggest to the problems of life, but because we believe it is life, not for aid in making the will of God prevail, but because we believe it is the will of God. We love it for its own sake . . ." Education, Dewey said, is not preparation for life: it *is* life! Intelligence, not knowledge, is the primary goal of education, though it is clear that without knowledge intelligence is impossible. But knowledge must have use, and that use must extend far beyond workplaces. Diane Ravitch (2010, 230) writes,

> Certainly we want them to be able to read and write and be numerate. Those are the basic skills on which all other learning builds. But that is not enough. We want to prepare them for a useful life. We want them to be able to think for themselves when they are out in the world on their own. We want them to have good character and to make sound decisions about their life, their work, and their health. We want them to face life's joys and travails with courage and humor. We hope that they will be kind and compassionate in their dealings with others. We want them to have a sense of justice and fairness. We want them to understand our nation and our world and the challenges we face. We want them to be active, responsible citizens, prepared to think issues through carefully, and to reach decisions rationally. We want them to learn science and mathematics so they understand the problems of modern life and participate in finding solutions. We want them to enjoy the rich artistic and cultural heritage of our society and other societies.

Our children must be made intelligent; that is to say, to learn *to think* about themselves and their worlds using the texts and materials that we can provide them in the schools. Our children must learn to think, in William James' formulation "*To sustain a* representation" (1892/1961, 320). Our children must be taught to imagine. It is the sustenance of the idea that leads to action. The alternative to this effort is passivity: the incapacity to sustain an idea is to lack will, and to leave our activities incomplete and unfinished, and be incapable of choice; to remain unwilling to act. In such a situation we lie abed unable to rise, or we await some else's command.

Teachers ought to be known as advocates of intelligence. To teachers is given the almost religious task of guarding and fostering intelligence. A story is told: the Rabbis wonder why there is so much sorrow among the Jews. Why, they ask, does the land perish and the people suffer? They complain that many scholars have been troubled by the question, but none has offered a reason for the desolation. Several Rabbis offer as response God's own response (Jeremiah 9:12) to the question: "Because they have forsaken my Torah which I set before them." That is, it would appear that the people's suffering derives from their having forsaken the ways of God, and the result has been punishment and suffering. In behaviorist terms, the cause and effect are eminently visible and clear.

But in fact the Rabbis have offered as rationale for the suffering only the first half of Jeremiah's statement; they purposely omitted the second half of God's ascribed response. The full statement in *Jeremiah* reads: "Because they have forsaken My Torah that I put before them, *they did not heed My voice nor follow it*" (italics added). I would suggest that by quoting only the first part of God's indictment the Rabbis have focused *not* on the people's descent into some iniquitous social behavior; rather, they are rebuked only for *forsaking* the Torah and not for disobeying it. That latter reproach is covered by the second part of the statement. Thus, the desolation of the land remains a mystery to them. And thus, the question of the land's desolation remains.

That is, in their explanation the Rabbis have eliminated the reference *to following* the teachings and focused on the people's stance toward it. Rav says that the hardships derive *not* from the *failure* to study, nor from any *decline* in the practice of the people's daily behavior. The Rabbis will accept neither that the people have behaved immorally nor even that study has precipitously declined in society. Rather, what Rav means by the *forsaking* of

Torah refers to the decline in the sacredness with which the people hold study! Rav says, actually quoting Rav Yehudah, that the suffering of the people continues "Because they did not recite the blessing for the Torah first." I consider Rav's response remarkable and apt. He asserts that the land is made forsaken because for the people study had become secular and not sacred. Study had lost its base in wonder and awe and had become mundane. Ordinary. Pro forma. Prosaic. Lifeless. You see, for the Rabbis study is not merely an essential and practical enterprise but also a holy one. Study is an engagement with the mysteries of the world. Study is a consecrated undertaking. The prayer before study sacralizes it. But, Rav asserts in the name of Rav Yehudah, the people have ceased offering blessings before and after study that would raise the event of study to the level of the holy. Hence, the land suffers because they have forsaken My Torah.

So, too, at present, is it in today's society: study partakes of little awe and wonder; rather, study is about measurement. And as a result, the land remains devastated. And for the repair of this condition, the endeavor of teachers is not simply necessary but essential because teachers have devoted their lives to the efficacy of learning, have immersed themselves in disciplines that they love *and* desire to share, and have dedicated themselves to sharing their passions with others in the hope of creating allies in their beliefs to inspire a better world, of provoking or feeding a curiosity that will become self-perpetuating, of inspiring the capacity to imagine: "a way of toying with, exploring, trying out new and sometimes farfetched ideas" (Walton, 1990, 22). Teachers are essential for opening the world of study to those who otherwise would not know its necessities and pleasures. Teachers prepare for the messiah by engaging themselves and others in acts of study and benevolence.

A depiction of the sacredness of study appears in an episode of *Joan of Arcadia*, a 2003–05 television show. In the episode "Saint Joan," the work of the teacher, Mr. Paul Dreisback, is made critical not simply for *what* he teaches but *that* he teaches. And though over the years Mr. Dreisback has experienced frustration and disappointment in the classroom, in this episode the efforts of his students' study renew him and allow him to take back his crown, as did the French under the leadership of Joan of Arc after their bitter defeat at Agincourt in 1415. Mr. Dreisback finally triumphs not merely for what he knows but for what he believes. In "Saint Joan" the sacredness of learning remains the focus: in this episode, study creates, and what transpires in this classroom between student and teacher is not information but awareness. In the show's penultimate scene, Mr. Dreisback admits that after thirty years of teaching he had begun to experience defeat in his classroom practice, going out not in a blaze of glory but "mired in the mud of my student's indifference." But in this episode Joan's mystifying and remarkable achievement encourages Mr. Dreisback. In the classroom darkened by afternoon shadows, Mr. Dreisback looks directly at Joan and acknowledges, "I made you care about history, Ms. Girardi. I don't know how I did it but I did. And that's the whole point. You inspired me to take back my crown." Joan announces to the family and its therapist in the show's final scene, "Well, I retook the test and I got an A. And I well, sort of saved someone's life." And indeed, it was two lives that Joan's actions had saved: Mr. Dreisback's and her own. In this episode, study has become sacred and saved lives. "You have no idea," Joan says to Mr. Dreisback, "how cool this is!" And he responds, "Oh yes, I do." In this episode, the land is made green again.

"Saint Joan" begins in a darkened high school classroom. Mr. Dreisback, a history teacher, is conducting his lesson on the Hundred Years' War (1337–1453) and the devastating defeat in 1415 of the French at the Battle of Agincourt. Shakespeare's *Henry V* will celebrate the English victory on that battlefield, though I have learned that a mock trial conducted in March 2010 (with Supreme Court Justices Samuel Alito and Ruth Bader Ginsburg among the judges) unanimously ruled that King Henry V's slaughter of French prisoners of war was legally unjustified; they awarded unspecified damages to the estates of the murdered prisoners. I do not think the behavior of Henry V was part of Mr. Dreisback's lesson; it was certainly not part of Shakespeare's play.

But to continue: the classroom is dark because the teacher is showing slides of the battle as he lectures, but from within the classroom there is the clear sound of one student, head pillowed on her arm on the desk, snoring rather volubly. As Mr. Dreisback droningly intones, Joan Girardi noisily sleeps. Provoked by his student's inattention, Mr. Dreisback raises the metal wastebasket and drops it noisily on the floor where its clangor awakens the slumbering Joan. "Huh, what?" she stammers, startled semi-alert from her slumber. Addressing to her a question concerning the matter through which she has slept, Mr. Dreisback asks, "What was the problem, Miss Girardi?" Of course, Joan hasn't a clue to what Mr. Dreisback refers: not only has she been sleeping through this class, but she has also clearly not read the assigned material. Joan is not and has never been a stellar student. Indeed, throughout the entire series Joan's marginal position as any sort of scholar remains central to her characterization. In this particular instance, it is another student, Mr. Dreisback's brown-nosed pet, Steven Zackheim, straining somewhat too enthusiastically to get himself called on from the very beginning, who impatiently responds to Mr. Dreisback's question. He trumpets out the answer, enigmatically: "Mud!" What Zackheim refers to concerns the weather conditions that impaired the movement of the French soldiers on the battlefield and led to their defeat at Agincourt. It seems that during the evening before the battle it had rained heavily, and the French soldiers dressed in their cumbersome armor became bogged down in the mud and were easily defeated by the less weighted and more motile English army. Joan finds herself so stuck in much the same way. So, too, we will learn, is Mr. Dreisback, "mired," as he will say, in the mud of his student's indifference. Joan's actions in the episode will renew both of them and offer each a taste of triumph and victory, and an engagement and understanding of the sacredness of study.

Now, the topic of Mr. Dreisback's pedagogical unit is not just this single battle of Agincourt, in fact, but also the entire Hundred Years' War (1337–1453), and so after establishing cause for the French defeat at Agincourt, Mr. Dreisback continues on with his lecture. As he proceeds, Mr. Dreisback describes the humiliating defeat of the French and the meteoric rise of Jeanne d'Arc, or as she is known in modern parlance, Joan of Arc, the young French girl who claimed to hear God's voice telling her to take back the French crown. It was she, says Mr. Dreisback, who saved the day for the French; it was her effort that helped restore the crown to Charles VII of France. And at Mr. Dreisback's reference to Joan of Arc, Joan of Arcadia sits up in her seat, awake, attentive, and focused.

Joan of Arcadia aired on television first in 2003 and was a contemporary version of the story of that same Joan of Arc who, upon hearing God's word, led the French to several military victories in the Hundred Years' War. In fact, Joan of Arc's actions helped restore the monarchy to France. Eventually captured, she was tried and convicted on a trumped up and politically motivated charge of heresy and was burned at the stake in 1431 when she was nineteen years old. Later, she was canonized as a saint. The contemporary Joan of Arcadia is a very ordinary middle-class sixteen-year-old high school student who inexplicably begins to receive regular visits and directives from God; in each episode God assumes a different persona when s/he calls upon Joan. The theme song of the show comes from Joan Osbourne: "What if God was one of us / Just a slob like one of us / Just a stranger on the bus / Trying to make his way home." Indeed, in the first episode of the show, it is on a public city bus that Joan hears from God. In each subsequent episode of *Joan of Arcadia* God appears to Joan as one of us, not only as either male or female but also as adult and child as well. Furthermore, during the course of any one episode, God takes on any appropriate human form so as to appear naturally to Joan as she proceeds through her very normal adolescent academic, social, and family life. That is, wherever Joan happens to be, there she might hear from God. In each episode God advises Joan to act in ways that are at odds with her daily routine and that usually even conflict with it. For example, in one episode God tells Joan *to get a job*; in another he insists that she *enroll in AP chemistry*, in a third he orders her *to learn to play chess*, and in others to *try out for the cheerleading squad, take her drivers test*, and *learn to jump rope*. Once, God even commands Joan *to build a boat*! And though Joan questions God's words, she nevertheless always follows God's lead. As a result of her actions, she changes herself and the world. That's the point.

"Saint Joan," the episode I address here, concerns education and learning, subjects in which I have spent my entire life. I am a teacher and a learner. Specifically, this episode focuses on the classroom, on teachers, and thematically on the necessity of learning *history* as essential knowledge for an understanding of the present. I agree heartily with the show's premise: for years I have myself attempted to always historicize, historicize, historicize, and I teach the necessity of this activity to students. At times I have even been somewhat effective. I think in this regard this episode of *Joan of Arcadia* serves the educational community well: it advocates for learning, for reading, and for study. In "Saint Joan," history derives its importance by giving meaning to the present and making change in it possible. In this episode, as in each of the episodes, Joan changes by following God's directives.

The problem stems, I believe, from the fact that Joan has not been learning history in Mr. Dreisback's class. Recall that at the show's opening she is in class fast asleep. Indeed, Mr. Dreisback's classroom, though seemingly functional, has become rather dull. In their final conference, Joan will say to Mr. Dreisback—a fact he will regretfully acknowledge—that except for Steve Zackheim, the teacher has reached no one in the class. As he will admit, of late he has been floundering in the mud of his students' indifference. The land is desolate because they have forsaken My Torah. In this particular episode, Joan attends to the lesson not due to

Mr. Dreisback's teaching but rather, due to his casual mention of Joan of Arc—Joan hears in Joan of Arc's story strong echoes of her own. Unbeknownst to Mr. Dreisback, when he talks about Joan of Arc he speaks also of Joan of Arcadia.

As Mr. Dreisback continues his narrative concerning the career of Joan of Arc, he asserts that though she claimed to have heard the words of God, modern psychoanalysts might have a different explanation for her behavior: they might describe Joan of Arc as a "paranoid schizophrenic with messianic tendencies." The strange visitations from God that Joan has experienced have identified Joan of Arcadia wholly with Joan of Arc, and when Mr. Dreisback intimates that Joan of Arc was crazy, the modern day Joan calls out almost in self-defense, "But she wasn't crazy," speaking, of course, of herself. When the teacher asks if Joan Girardi has a different explanation, the bell rings, and the class ends with the announcement that Wednesday's test on this unit will be short answer and count for *fifty percent* of the term's grade. Indeed, at the moment, Joan has no other explanation but she is, as it were, saved by the bell. She remains, however, visibly troubled by the topic.

Mr. Dreisback has no insight into Joan's intense response, but then, who would? At a dinner conversation Joan startles even her family with the vehemence of her defense of Joan of Arc. "Joan of Arc wasn't crazy," she insists during a casual conversation inspired by her studious reading at the dinner table of Butler's *Lives of the Saints*. For what concerns Joan Girardi is the idea that if Joan of Arc was, indeed, crazy—"a paranoid schizophrenic with messianic tendencies"—then so too might she be mad. After all, Joan talks to God who tells her to act in certain ways and accomplish particular things. Joan does, indeed, it seems to me, have much to be concerned with regarding the manner in which Mr. Dreisback has characterized Joan of Arc. And among other issues, this characterization concerns history: the French soldiers who followed her, after all, did not think her mad; history, in the perspective of

Mr. Dreisback, however, has not been so kind to Joan of Arc, and this circumstance unsettles Joan of Arcadia in the present.

As she walks to school the next morning Joan remains deeply troubled by the subject of Joan of Arc's sanity: she wonders to her friend, Grace Polk, if Grace considers that Joan of Arc was crazy, though Joan's understanding of class discussion yet remains somewhat imprecise. Recall, Joan is not a stellar student, and so she wonders to Grace if Mr. Dreisback's characterization of Joan of Arc as "a paranoid schizophrenic with a miscellaneous complex" is accurate. Grace suggests that the word Joan seeks is "messianic." "Whatever," responds Joan, "but do you think she was crazy?" But by this time Grace has become bored with the conversation—she admits, "I'm no poster child for sanity"—and walks quickly on toward the building, leaving Joan behind. It is at this moment, as Joan stands seemingly abandoned, that God—this time in the persona of a groundskeeper trimming a tree in front of the school building—calls down to her from atop his ladder under a tree: "You're not crazy, Joan." And then God, climbing down the ladder from his work in the tree, says to Joan, "You know this history test? I want you to ace it." Joan complains: "That's unsettling when God uses slang. Do you mean you want me to get an A? But I hate history, and this is the One Hundred Years War which is really long . . . History is so over!" The groundskeeper, God, looks about him on the ground and notes aloud that because the tree had not been trimmed the previous year, the branches had become so overgrown that the grass underneath it had died and now the entire area will need to be reseeded. Joan shrugs and says, "This whole metaphor thing is a real pain." She wonders if perhaps God couldn't be more clear and direct. But then Joan, yet anxious about her own sanity, asks God if he had really spoken to Joan of Arc, and whether she really was crazy. But in response God merely reiterates his directive: "Get an A on the test, Joan," and climbs back up the ladder to continue his work. God does not provide an answer but only the opportunity to pursue questions. "You know," she calls in her frustration, "a lot of people don't like you." Nevertheless, Joan will do God's bidding. Her behavior will define for her God's metaphor.

That metaphor God has provided but that yet held no meaning to Joan suggested that history *is* important because without history we act as if we were alone and without context—the grass died because someone did not pay attention to the natural process— and that this violence resulted from not knowing history. Emmanuel Levinas (1990) has said that "violence is to be found in any action in which one acts as if one were alone to act: as if the rest of the universe were there only to receive the action. Violence is consequently also any action which we endure without at every point collaborating in it" (p. 6). Violence, it is suggested, stems from a willed ignorance. God insists that Joan must learn something about history even as she must learn some history; for Joan God's ways are always mysterious but, as she comes to understand, they have ethical value. God's directive to Joan demands that she learn something, though God's insistence in this instance remains a mystery to Joan. "I hate history," she whines. The episode will offer Joan a wholly new perspective on the subject.

More significantly perhaps, God takes advantage of Joan's personal concern about the characterization of Joan of Arc's mental state, and Joan's absorption with Saint Joan sends her to books for information: she demands to learn about Joan of Arc because she must come to some awareness of herself. It is not the One Hundred Years' War that concerns Joan of Arcadia, though it is that conflict that has been the subject of Mr. Dreisback's class. Joan's rigorous study for the test focuses almost wholly on the life of Joan of Arc. Joan of Arcadia is personally engaged in the subject because the subject is her life. For Mr. Dreisback's test she does not study from the course textbook nor from the notes that clearly she has not taken; rather, she does her reading at the local bookstore at which she is employed (the result of an earlier directive from God). Joan sits at a reading table behind a towering stack of books, most seemingly about the life of Joan of Arc. She asks the proprietor for help with her work, but he tells her to *"read the books."* He adds, "I have a Master's Degree in English Literature. I could have done a number of things with my life . . . but I chose to open a bookstore because I believe in the power of knowledge that comes from books. You want to learn something? Read!" In this case, Joan of Arcadia demands *for very personal reasons* to understand the life and character of Joan of Arc. Joan of Arcadia reads, and the owner of the bookstore has wisely advised her to make the necessary effort herself.

On the day of the test, Mr. Dreisback hands out the test papers and mockingly expresses his hope that Miss Girardi has slept well, and Joan responds with not a little disdain, "Not very well. I was up late reading history." Mr. Dreisback conveys some skepticism, but Joan insists, "I *did* study. And I learned stuff! Like Joan of Arc wasn't schizo, for example. And they didn't kill her for saying that she heard voices. They killed her for wearing pants. The trial was totally corrupt. She was a scapegoat . . . " The entire class has by this time sat up in their seats startled first, that Joan seems to know something—anything at all, actually—and shocked as well at the aggressive nature of her response to her teacher. Apparently, this is behavior uncharacteristic of Joan of Arcadia. Mr. Dreisback insists, "Tell me on the test, Joan," but she adds, arrogantly and *sotto voce*, "You're teaching the whole thing wrong." At this comment, the tension in the room increases excruciatingly, but Joan continues, "Well, what really happened is these bossy judges forced her to wear pants in the courtroom, made it look like she was a witch, which totally gave them permission to fry her." Zackheim asks if Joan's emendations to the story of Joan of Arc will be on the test. Mr. Dreisback looks up and says, "Don't ask me, apparently my authority counts for nothing." He returns to the seat at his desk in the front of the room, but he stares out at Joan startled and stung at her riposte.

The test over, Joan leaves the building and takes a seat on the bench at the local bus stop in front of the school. God (this time in the form of a young woman knitting and also waiting for a bus) reprimands Joan for her discourteous counter to Mr. Dreisback, for the violence of her response to him in the classroom. Sitting on the bus bench God narrates to Joan something about Mr. Dreisback's history, telling her that in his youth Mr. Dreisback had played the saxophone and turned down a scholarship to study music at Julliard so that he might become a teacher: he was *passionate about history and wanted to share his passion with others.* Interestingly enough, God here points out that it is not the subject of history that is significant so much as is Mr. Dreisback's *passion* for history. The source of that passion remains unexplored save that it is such that he felt compelled to share it.

Studying history, God had earlier said, was essential for managing the present. But despite her concern for Joan of Arc—or rather, in ignorance of its historical nature—Joan rejects God's narration of Mr. Dreisback's history in order to maintain her comfortable current perspective of both he and his subject. To God Joan sarcastically quips that to put passion and Mr. Dreisback in the same sentence is unsettling. God responds, "If you make snap judgments about people and are unwilling to look into their pasts, you'll never begin to understand them." This is the overt theme of the show's focus on history; recall God's earlier metaphor. But Joan rejects God's advice, refusing the nature of the very history that she has consumed in order to understand *herself.* "He's a dweeb," Joan accuses, and God answers, "He's your teacher!" Joan responds, "I don't like him," and rising from the bench to get on the arriving bus, God answers her, "You don't have to like him. Let him teach you." At this bus stop God has offered us some necessary insight: we learn that Mr. Dreisback had become a teacher because he wanted to share his passion and not his subject, though of course the two are not unconnected. Interestingly, Joan will learn not from Mr. Dreisback but from her experience with him, even as Mr. Dreisback will learn from his experience with Joan. Both will come to a new understanding of history and themselves, and both will come to appreciate the holiness of study.

I don't care about the illogicalities in the show: we have seen Joan surrounded by so many books that it is difficult to accept that she has had the time to read even one of them, much less all of them, in the day or two between the interchange in the classroom and the test. Nothing has ever suggested that Joan was a stellar student. Mr. Dreisback tells Joan to tell him her knowledge on the test, but the short answer nature of the test precludes any narrative. Student Zackheim's question concerning Joan's revisions in Joan of Arc's story being material that might be on the test is absurd because, in fact, the new information came not from Mr. Dreisback but from Joan: this material couldn't possibly be on the exam which Mr. Dreisback hands out to the class. However, for the sake of the plot the question *is* necessary to make possible Joan's barbed retort and Mr. Dreisback's wounded reaction; Joan must speak haughtily, even insolently, to her teacher to enable not only the story line to proceed but to give meaning to God's earlier metaphor. Joan in her study learned some history, but she has a great deal more to understand.

Because she has been provoked by the insinuations made about the mental stability of Joan of Arc with whom she personally identifies, Joan has studied intensively for the test on the Hundred Years' War, though it is mostly the integrity of Joan of Arc that has been the object of study for Joan of Arcadia. And as God had demanded, Joan earns an A+ on the test. But neither Mr. Dreisback nor Assistant Principal Mr. Price believe that Joan could have earned that A without cheating: a C- being the highest grade she had scored thus far in history, and they demand that she retake the test, "to level the playing field," as they say. Of course, Joan is outraged by their insinuations, and she refuses to retake the exam. As does her namesake, Joan chooses to battle the oppressor, and she becomes the center of a protest movement organized mostly by her politically active friend Grace; *No Proof, No Test* the posters and buttons read. The "rebellion" galvanizes the school and threatens to divide it. Students who continue the protest are threatened with suspension. But Joan, like Joan of Arc, remains adamant and refuses to bow to authority, until in the character of a custodial painter in the school, God tells Joan to abandon the crusade and her cloak of martyrdom and to retake the test. This episode, apparently, is not about revolt and injustice. This program is about study, history, and redemption. Joan retakes the test.

And so in the final scene of the show, Mr. Dreisback calls Joan into his yet-dark classroom and returns the retest on which she has earned another A+. "Wow!" says Joan. Mr. Dreisback then sits down in the desk beside her and thanks Joan: he says that though he has taught for thirty years, he has of late become disheartened and lost his enthusiasm for the classroom. "Somewhere along the line I got discouraged and started phoning it in," he admits. Of course, this Mr. Dreisback suffers from a condition familiarly known as teacher burn-out. As he says, it is a teacher's greatest fear! And what has discouraged him was the apparent absence in his students of any evidence of his own passion for history. Mr. Dreisback's students don't seem to care about the subject as he has cared for it, as he wished them to care for it. He has experienced failure. Mr. Dreisback tells Joan that prior to this incident with her he had decided "to quit—I wasn't going out in a blaze of glory but I was surrendering in defeat like the French at Agincourt." Mr. Dreisback attributes this classroom failure to the indifference of the students, though by definition indifference occurs only in relationship. Hence, Mr. Dreisback is culpable, as I think he understands. And then he says, "But I made you care about history, Miss Girardi, I don't know how I did it, but I made you care about history. And that's the whole point . . . You inspired me to take back my crown." Of course, his metaphor references the achievement of Joan of Arc's victories in the wars against the

English and the return of the crown to the French king deposed by Henry V's victory at Agincourt. And then, with tears in his eyes (and a few in Joan's) Mr. Dreisback says, "I thank you." You see, it was herself Joan discovered in history, and it was history Joan found in discovering herself. The program enacts the perfect Deweyan pedagogy: Joan became her learning and her learning became Joan. Concerned about being Joan of Arc, she becomes Joan of Arcadia, and in the process restores Mr. Dreisback to himself. The whole point to which Mr. Dreisback refers is the concern, even passion, for learning that Joan has exhibited: learning has become again sacred.

The program advocates for knowledge and for reading. "You want to learn something, read!" Well, that's one answer, and to my mind a rather good one, but to read well one needs must first have a question for which one seeks answers. This particular episode of the show concerns the essential nature to our lives of the knowledge of history that Joan derives from her reading. Of this, too, I could not be more supportive. But Joan doesn't just read history for the sake of reading nor does she study for the sake of studying and "acing the test": she has something she must learn about her life, and she has a very specific question for which she searches for answers. She is *learning* history but she is not *studying* history. In fact, Joan's interest concerns the psychological stability of Joan of Arc and not Joan of Arc's place in history, though certainly the former issue is subsumed in the latter one. And it is Joan of Arcadia with whom Joan is concerned and not the very long Hundred Years' War. She has learned what God had earlier avowed: that a concern for the past determines the present.

The life that Joan saved was, in fact, her own. Joan of Arcadia has some personal stake in Joan of Arc, and no one but Joan of Arcadia could understand this connection. How could they? Therefore, Joan Girardi's intense interest in Joan of Arc can*not* be attributed to Mr. Dreisback's teaching: ironically, Joan's learning does *not* occur as a result of Mr. Dreisback's passion; rather, Joan's learning derives from her own passion. By his own admission Mr. Dreisback's passion has since faded, and as Joan admits to him, perhaps, he has reached only the student Steve Zackheim. But when Mr. Dreisback offers his support to the theory that Joan of Arc was crazy, unbeknownst to him, he has assigned the same disordered mental state to Joan of Arcadia, and to save herself Joan must redeem Joan of Arc. And to do so she must read. In Mr. Dreisback's class Joan finds something she did not even know she had lost. And in the process of this discovery, Joan learns the history she had earlier disparaged. Mr. Dreisback is incorrect to think that Joan's grade on the test was inspired by his teaching. Joan's story is made possible by her passion to know history for very personal reasons which finally no one but Joan knows. Joan's remarkably concerted engagement in study occurs *in spite* of Mr. Dreisback's uninspired and uninspiring teaching. Though Mr. Dreisback assumes the critical role in her learning, albeit admitting ignorance of how he achieved this feat, Joan pursues knowledge because it is herself about whom she is concerned! When Mr. Dreisback says that he didn't know how he did it, he speaks more truth than he knows. Indeed, ironically, Mr. Dreisback inspired Joan by denying everything he knew about history—he has denied the possibility of an alternate story. He has, indeed, become stuck in the mud not of his student's indifference but of his own emotional disquiet.

A story is told (Buber, 1991, 314): Once there was a man who was very stupid. Every morning when he arose, it was so hard for him to find his clothes that at night he almost hesitated to go to bed for thinking of the trouble he would have on waking to find his clothes. One evening he finally made a great effort, and as he took off each piece of clothing he noted down on a piece of paper exactly where he had put everything that he had just taken off. The next morning the man arose, and pleased with himself, he took the slip of paper in hand and read: "cap"—and there it was, and he set it on his head; "pants"—there they lay, and he put them on, one leg at a time. So it went until finally he was fully dressed. The man turned to the mirror: "That's all very well, but now, where am I myself? Where in the world am I?" You see, all the man knew was the clothes he put on, and not the man on whom the clothes were put. So it was with Joan and her studies: she could put on the clothes, but had no idea where she was herself *until* the historical became personal. Too often education has been the compiling of lists of where we have put on our clothes and it has ignored the person on whom the clothes should be put. In this episode Joan Girardi learns, through history, who and where she is in the world.

Joan of Arcadia becomes Saint Joan by restoring Mr. Dreisback's faith in himself as a teacher. And concurrently, Joan becomes Joan of Arcadia by discovering the presence of her own sanity and her capacity for learning. In this classroom and in this particular situation, it is Joan Girardi's passion that restores Mr. Dreisback's enthusiasm for teaching and for history. It is her effort that causes him to learn. Here, ironically, the teacher's failure produces the student's success.

Of course, Joan's accomplishment on this one history test does not portend her transformation into a stellar student. Indeed, she remains to the end of the series an "average student." That isn't the point, really, and I really don't know how to adequately define an "average student." But the program suggests that learning occurs regardless of the teacher when that learning ties the individual to the world. The classroom should be a place where the student engages in study and in study encounters herself; the classroom should be the place where she might encounter and engage with the world in the enactment of that study.

CHAPTER 5

THE LAST LESSON

FOR YEARS, DURING STRESSFUL TIMES I HAVE TURNED WITH THOUGHT and ear to Sydney Carter's hymn-like song, "Julian of Norwich." The lyric derives from the words of Julian of Norwich, a fourteenth-century anchoress and mystic. I have always taken great comfort from her counsel:

> All shall be well I'm telling you
> Let the winter come and go
> All shall be well again, I know.

I recall once singing that song to a student who was about to undergo a delicate brain surgery that would attempt to control his severe epilepsy. More recently I sent the song to my own child who was suffering a broken heart. In both cases, I hoped that the words served some solace. We all need a little comfort sometimes.

A story was told: The wise King Solomon owned a ring on which he had engraved the words "This too shall pass." Whenever events turned against him and he suffered in defeat and depression, he would look at the ring and read, "This too shall pass," and he was comforted. And when fortune appeared favorable to him and his kingdom, then also would he look at the ring: "This too shall pass," and he was comforted. Solomon's ring reminded him of the ephemeral and temporary nature of life. He was wise to attend to the ring because from it he would know to ever be prepared for a turn of events. He was always expectantly ready, though he must not have been always pleased as events unfolded.

And again: In *Waiting for Godot* Vladimir says, "The tears of the world are a constant quantity." When one stops her weeping, then somewhere another begins to cry. Vladimir suggests that the level of sorrow neither increases nor decreases: though it may variously occupy different sites, the degree of sorrow in the world stays constant. And I understand in Vladimir's words an expression of Solomonic wisdom: if the tears of the world are a constant quantity, then this difficulty for me, too, shall pass. I am comforted.

I believe that it requires a great deal of courage to take these daily stances in the world. No one would wish the end of their happiness, nor can one easily foresee a cessation to their sorrow. A certain stoicism is required in either situation. Seneca (2004, 67) writes, "It is in times of security that the spirit should be preparing itself to deal with difficult times; while fortune is bestowing favours on it then is the time for it to be strengthened against her rebuffs." I think rarely—and perhaps, least of all today—has the teacher, a community to which I proudly belong, time for respite or security. We teachers are and have been for some time sorely beset. Nevertheless, we keep on keeping on. We can be heroes.

In her functioning the teacher assumes this stoic stance daily. Standing before her classes, she appears as the person who knows, but if she is very wise, then she knows that she doesn't for certain know. Her charge is to educate, but what that means is too often defined by others who do not in fact know what she does know, and who without cause have little confidence in her capacity to fulfill her task. Indeed, the teacher knows that though she teaches, some of her students still might not learn through absolutely no fault of her own and sometimes not even of theirs. She is constrained to be silent though she must speak. And at the end of the day she returns home wondering what had transpired today, what had she done, what value had she added. She reads in the newspapers or hears on the televisions and radios that the problem with America lies in her incompetence. She wonders if this sorrow too will pass, but the news continues to remain negative. And though polls report that most parents love their local school, the same polls report that few approve of the school system as a whole (http://pdkintl.org/wp-content/blogs.dir/5/files/2012-Gallup-poll-full-report.pdf). Books attacking public schools, teachers, and teachers' unions pop up overnight like poisonous mushrooms, and the government initiatives, policies, and programs offer little respite and yet more critique. Public schools compete with unsuccessful charter schools for the ever-decreasing funds that state governments have allocated for public education, thus condemning those very schools and the teachers who work in them to inadequate resources and insufficient recompense for the difficult job they have undertaken. Too many who occupy the schools walk about with their spiritual and intellectual lives at risk. Fifty percent of teachers quit the field after five years, many of them from having been too badly beaten. It is difficult to believe that all shall be well again or that this too shall pass.

There are almost 3.5 million public school teachers in the United States; there are perhaps another 60,000–70,000 more teachers in private and independent schools and almost 1.7 million teachers in higher education. And almost daily I hear someone who is not engaged in the schools or education decry the incompetence of so many of these teachers. Since at least 1983 and *A Nation at Risk*, teachers have been the object of the vitriol of the politicians and businessmen in the United States. Everyone who has no knowledge of education and teaching but assigns a great political (or economic) interest to it has weighed in on the poor quality of the whole system, commenting particularly and viciously on the ineffectiveness, nay, the incompetence of the teachers. And too many of those teachers skulk about almost ashamed that what they are accused of is true. And *that* is a terrible shame. As the school doors open I see too many teachers steal through them shamefacedly; they have been labeled the enemy and their efforts maligned and condemned. Teachers truly are at risk. And the accusation? It is they who have caused the imperial decline in the United States, it is they who produced the economic downturn, and they who have caused and ill-fought two wars. The decline of the cities, the return of segregated education, the growing gap between rich and poor is lain at the feet of the incompetent teachers. The leash tightens. It is all an appalling, malodorous lie. Shall all be well again?

Rules and regulations and core standards proliferate and are handed down to teachers on an almost daily basis. They adhere to the regulations in anticipation and desperation. Common Core Standards. Standardized testing. The National Council for the Accreditation of Teacher Education (NCATE). And now edTPA. There is little opportunity to learn, we are too busy teaching what they say we must teach, administering too many tests that they require. Czeslaw Milosz (1981, xiii) writes: "A man may persuade himself, by the most logical reasoning, that he will greatly benefit his health by swallowing live frogs; and, thus rationally convinced, he may swallow a first frog, then the second; but at the third his stomach will revolt." Teachers give up, give in, and many get out and stay out. I am afraid they have eaten too many live frogs. Theirs is made an impossible task: to teach what will not be learned and to advocate for what should not or cannot be learned.

Teachers are aware that knowledge is not the product we offer in the classroom but the ability acquired there to further pursue learning. Teachers understand that knowledge is not a product to be gained but a process in which to be engaged. Study is a stance we assume in the world. In his essay "Walking," Thoreau distinguishes between knowledge and what he refers to as Sympathy with Intelligence. He writes, "I do not know that this higher knowledge amounts to anything more definite than a novel and grand surprise on a sudden revelation of the insufficiency of all that we called Knowledge before—a discovery that there are more things in heaven and earth than are dreamed of in our philosophy" (2001, 250). As Thoreau suggested, study is a way of being—it is an ethics. When we learn we acknowledge in public our sense of wonder and awe. Wonder is a radical amazement; wonder is a state of maladjustment to words and notions, the recognition of their fluidity. Wonder arises in the awareness of the world's glory that always exceeds our comprehension and our grasp.

We respond to our wonder with awe. To experience awe is to acknowledge that there is meaning in the smallest particle, if only we could understand. In an article concerning the current state of knowledge in physics, Steven Weinberg acknowledges, "The history of elementary particle physics has followed a very different course from that of cosmology. Rather than being starved for data fifty years ago, we were deluged by data we could not understand" (2013, 87). Despite the great advances in our knowledge that has over the years occurred, Weinberg (2013, 88) cautions, "Physical science has historically progressed not only by finding precise explanations of natural phenomena, but also by discovering what sorts of things *can* be precisely explained. These may be fewer than we had thought." In the tradition of study we acknowledge how little we know. We stand in awe at the complexities of our lives that we only realize in part. Study offers us moments of insight and chances for direction. Study is the awareness that we live amidst daily miracles, and that there is more to the world than we will ever know. Abraham Joshua Heschel (1959, 52) writes that "The beginning of awe is wonder, and the beginning of wisdom is awe." Study is an expression of awe. When we study we take a stance in awe and humility, and we actively acknowledge that "our lives take place under horizons that range beyond the span of an individual life, or even the life of a generation, a nation, or an era." Study emanates from the silence of awe and wonder. If contemporary chaos theory argues that there is order in the universe but that it is only recognizable in time, then engagement in study acknowledges our patience and our hope. Knowledge, Heschel teaches, is fostered by curiosity (52). Study might set standards to which we aspire but never reach. It is not for lack of trying that the standards cannot be achieved; it is that the standards always elude us. They are a consummation devoutly to be sought for but never achieved. Not a school district in the United States exists that does not contain in its mission statement the intent to create life-long learners, but every school-year learning ends with the tests they administer. How many frogs can one teacher eat?

I have learned to accept that education in our schools today has little to do with learning, a process that I believe ought to be continual and difficult and that could be boundless, but that has today become only that which, with exactly focused behavioral objectives and measured, standardized achievement, sets firmly bounded and clearly defined ends. In schools today, the answer must be readily available, repeatable, and testable. Students are taught to ask, "What did I get?" and never to wonder, "What did I give?" There are finite classes of carefully scripted materials that are circumscribed by exact beginning and ending dates: at the former one is presented with a syllabus and at the latter assigned a grade. The teacher is required to prepare every class so that it arrives at a definite conclusion that will lead directly to the next day's lesson and that follows immediately from that of the previous one. "What does education often do? It makes a straight-cut ditch of a free, meandering brook" Thoreau complains. And so at the semester's end another check mark may be made to the credit audit report and another step toward graduation marked completed. The teacher files away her syllabus and class notes, and then it is on to the next course. I have been told *ad nauseam* that my role as teacher will be assessed by the value that is added to the student as a result of the experience of my class, but I don't know how to establish the character of that value by which I will be adjudged except by the standardized texts by which I refuse to be bounded and in which I cannot believe. My stomach turns at the third frog.

There is something sterile about education today in this age of accountability, and something quite deadening to the lives of the teachers who choose to enter the classroom that are governed by these measures. These teachers are constrained, however, to attend to the dictates and initiatives of those in power in order to maintain their position in what ought to be an honorable profession but has become a mere rote service-for-hire. Too often the teacher rationally eats the first and even the second frog. In few classrooms are teachers responsible for teaching that learning has no end, or that learning ought to engage students in the mire and the muck of life rather than keep them secluded from it. I suspect that a better awareness of this adventure might prepare students for the lives they will inevitably live in the world. Our tests and accountability assessments falsify the complexity of the world *and* the world of learning, and thereby, they avoid the difficult task of education. Tests and common core standards have become the standardized answer, but I wonder to what question they are a response. Too often I think we teach rather to listen without thought and to say by rote. I think that in the schools we have ceased standing in awe of the world that surrounds us. I think rather, that the world too often terrifies us, and our standards and certainties assuage our fear. Nevertheless, these answers have become precarious constraints. Berlin (2000, 16) warns, "To force people into the neat uniforms demanded by dogmatically believed-in schemes is almost always the road to inhumanity. We can only do what we can: but that we must do, against difficulties." The stomach of the wise and heroic teacher turns as she attempts to swallow the third frog: she refuses.

Not a Digression

I have been watching reruns of *Scrubs*, a television situation comedy that ran from 2001 through 2010. In the opening sequence the main characters serially pass to each other an X-ray negative that intern J.D. eventually hangs on a backlight box and that names the show's title. In the background the opening jingle declares, "I can't do this all on my own. No, I'm no superman," and refers clearly not only to the series of doctors who have passed along the X-ray photograph, but to the nature of the entire medical profession. It is an interesting admission that suggests that despite the comedic aspects of the show, all will not be well enough. Indeed, in season four, Resident Director Dr. Perry Cox, standing before a new contingent of interns, offers what was promoted as a supportive pep talk. He speaks with enthusiasm and excitement: "Okay, here it is. Every one of you is going to kill a patient. At some point . . . you will screw up, they will die, and it will be burned into your consciousness forever." Needless to say, he terrifies the neophytes! I teach that episode to first year students in the teacher education program at the university who arrive to class with some vague, romantic motive for becoming a teacher, and who hold some idealized image of the work teaching entails. *Their* teacher *is* the superman and I work to disabuse them of this myth and provide them with a method to hold off their first kill. But Cox continues, "The harder you study the longer you may be able to hold off that first kill." It is little comfort but it offers some relief and motive.

Our educational standards today mask the risks and difficulties that are intrinsic to the position of teacher. Our objective in education has become not to learn, a pursuit that demands the commission of error after error, but to be right, a condition that assumes no mistake! As Thoreau earlier suggested, the acceptance of uncertainty is the hallmark of intelligence, and it ought to be the teacher's work to prepare students to be at ease with ambiguity.

In Philip Roth's *American Pastoral* (1997, 35), Zuckerman says, "The fact remains that getting people right is not what living is all about anyway. It's getting them wrong that is living, getting them wrong and wrong and wrong and then, on careful reconsideration, getting them wrong again. That's how we know we're alive: we're wrong." Being wrong is the impetus to move forward. But in schools we penalize harshly for erroneous responses! Dewey somewhere says that an experiment whose results turn out as expected has been a badly designed experiment: there is nothing to think about if everything worked as planned. There is nothing to think about in the absolute achievement of success except the past.

In education we have been commanded to be right, but I do not think that that is how learning occurs. Learning requires problems, even insolvable ones, as Weinberg has suggested is the lesson of physics. We teachers? Well we're *no* supermen, either. Every one of us is going to kill a patient. When Ishmael heads out to sea it is because he is a seeker, and it is in the life at sea that he searches for "the image of the ungraspable phantom of life; and this is the key to it all." Ungraspable! Thoreau picks up a stoppered bottle that had washed up on the shore of Cape Cod (2004, 92) yet half full with red ale, and lifting it, as did Hamlet contemplating Yorick's skull, Thoreau says, "[A]s I poured it slowly onto the sand, it seemed to me that man himself was like a half-emptied bottle of pale ale, which Time had drunk so far, yet stoppled tight for a while, and drifting about in the ocean of circumstances; but destined erelong to mingle with the surrounding waves, or be spilled amid these sands of the distant shore." In Thoreau's words there is only the clear and singular sound of life's tragic view that today's classroom obscures behind a plethora of answers, numbers, and instruments of measurement.

I think that the sterility of contemporary classrooms organized by strict objectives and methods of assessment avoids the messiness of the world and cannot prepare students for the challenging and often difficult business of learning and teaching: I am a teacher and, at present, a teacher of teachers. Once (if not always) I was a high school English teacher. Doubt and ambiguity were my métier; these states were my entrance into thought and my strength in method, and I think it served my students well. But today, we hide our fears of chaos and disorder—of the certainty of uncertainty—behind all of the numbers and common core standards and instruments of assessments we employ to protect us from the void. We have stopped teaching for the ease of management and the safety and comfort of certainty.

What is't I do, in fact? This is not a casual question, for almost every day for the past forty-five years I have walked into the classroom as a teacher. What did I do? What should I have done? Despite the implication of the characterizations in the recent documentary, I am no superman, but in the eyes of society I have become in some odd way rendered superhumanly responsible for the current and future state of the whole country, at least. I have learned that this is my state because the description and directive appears daily in the newspapers. They—the politicians and pundits—say that my effort should result in a recovered world, a redeemed world. They say: my work should be such as to raise the dead. Alas, I recognize I am more like Herman Melville's Bartleby in "Bartleby, the Scrivener"; though standing on the green grass, I am yet encased in the Tombs: I know where I am.

What is to be done? What is't I do? I study and I teach, I teach and I study, and for my health, I forgo eating live frogs. The Rabbis wonder when the Messiah will come. *That* the Messiah will come never seems to them in doubt, but in the meantime, they acknowledge, we must yet continue to act. What should be the work done while waiting? What should be that work we do while we await the Messiah's arrival? In their discussion in *Sanhedrin,* the Rabbis turn to Scriptures to identify the time of the Messiah's arrival. Rab asserts that, "The son of David [the Messiah] will not come until the [Roman] power enfolds Israel for nine months." To arrive at this conclusion, Rab interprets a line from the prophet, Micah: V, 2: "God will deliver [Israel] to its enemies until the time that a woman in childbirth gives birth; then the rest of his brothers will return with the children of Israel." The statement means that the Messiah will come only after the Roman power has subjugated Israel completely—that is, in all of those lands to which the people of Israel are exiled—for as long as a woman is pregnant—nine months. Ulla responds, and Rabba agrees, "Let [the Messiah] come but let me not see him." Abaye wonders aloud, what might be Rabba's reason for not wishing to see the coming of the Messiah? Could it be, Abaye wonders, that Rabba does not wish to see the birth pangs—the difficulties and pains that precede the birth of a new era? And from the back of the room a timid student, one of Rabbi Eleazar's disciples, asks, "What must a man do to be spared the pangs [which precede the coming] of the Messiah?" Isn't there anything one can do to avoid the difficulties of this sight?" And Eleazar, his teacher, answers, "Let him engage in study and benevolence."

It is a curious answer. But I think it addresses the crisis in education which we daily confront. We teachers must wait for no deliverer, though there is no end to the claims of false Messiahs. Ralph Tyler. Madelyn Hunter. E. D. Hirsch. Arne Duncan. Diane Ravitch. William Bennett. Joel Klein. George W. Bush. Michael Bloomberg. Things *are* breaking up out there, Reb Dylan tells us. Perhaps they always have been: Parmenides seemed to think so. Our buildings are falling down and crumbling in decay. Soldiers besiege us. We teachers must await no savior. In our work, we teachers must ourselves become our succor. For it seems to me that the Rabbis have taught us what we must do while waiting; a waiting which itself would create conditions for the Messiah. We teachers must ourselves be our saviors. We must *study* and perform acts of *benevolence*. We must teach study and not always be studied. And this study is not a quietistic retreat into the ivory tower of the academy; rather, it is a study that is linked to acts of benevolence. Interestingly enough, Cox's lecture to the new interns ends in a similar directive: "The harder you study the longer will hold off your first kill." Study and benevolence. I'm no superman!

Let me approach my thoughts concerning the character and work of the teacher by another route. In Beckett's *Waiting for Godot*, Vladimir and Estragon hear Pozzo's cries for help and wonder what those cries oblige them to do. Vladimir says to Estragon, "To all mankind they were addressed, those cries for help still ringing in our ears! But at this place, at this moment of time, all mankind is us, whether we like it or not. Let us make the most of it, before it is too late! Let us represent worthily for once the foul brood to which a cruel fate consigned us!" I take some (but not full) exception to Vladimir's description of humanity as an unwholesome litter destined for base purpose. But hearing Pozzo's entreaties, Vladimir acknowledges to Estragon their obligations to the cries of distress that have been addressed, albeit, to all, but which they alone are present to hear: we should act, he urges Estragon. Of course, Vladimir and Estragon were not waiting for Pozzo; they were waiting for Godot (ah!), but Pozzo at this moment is representative of all humanity in need, and it is to Vladimir and Estragon that his cries are made and it is them that his cries oblige. Though Vladimir and Estragon have *not* set as their purpose to be responsible, circumstances have become such that they have the opportunity to act responsibly. They can do something![1]

Every time a teacher walks into the classroom she hears those cries for help ringing in her ears, even in the deadening silence of too many classrooms. But teachers *do* do something, and though they are far from perfect, they study harder to hopefully put off that first kill. It is *this* courage that makes teachers not supermen but heroes.

What is't we do? In this era of standardized high-stakes tests and constant measurement, this question persists: How to hear the cries addressed to all mankind and to know how to act when we hear them! Indeed, amidst the maddening crowd how may we hear our own cries? What is it that we would hear? Perhaps what we might hear in our classrooms is Pozzo's cries as he lies helplessly on the ground: "Help me rise!" It is very difficult work despite the ideology that says that teaching is easy. As David Labaree (2010) says, "In many ways, teaching is the most difficult of professions." To begin with, Labaree suggests, teachers depend on students for their success and there is only a minimum of control a teacher has over any one student's learning engagement. Second, students are mostly conscripts in the classroom: many are in school not because they want to learn or even understand how learning might be defined, but because by law, they must attend. Third, says Labaree, teachers need to carry out their practices under conditions of high uncertainty: what exactly is a teacher responsible for doing? Also, there exist these entities referred to as best practices, but that process assumes, I think, the presence of a patient etherized upon a table—a certain knowledge that the gall bladder must be removed, and a single best method to get it done. But I do not think that teaching works that way: at the least in the classrooms it is because the patient is awake, often resistant, and expected to participate *during* the process in some conscious relationship with the teacher. It is an unlikely combination even on a good day: and there are thirty students sitting before the teacher and not merely a single accommodating and unconscious patient. Cox says to the interns, "I know you're scared . . . But here's the dirty little secret: fear is good. It keeps you from becoming a crappy doctor. But you can't let [the fear] paralyze you!" To avoid hearing our fears or Pozzo's cries, many of us are instructed to turn up the music or don noise-cancellation earphones; we accede to the mandates handed down from administrative agencies who remain sensitive to the politicos whose agenda is reelection and not education. We are offered for consumption another live frog. Some of us even swallow it.

 I think that the strict standards and organized procedures that now govern our classrooms render silent and invisible the complexity of experience with which teachers daily must contend and for which they must prepare students. Too often this adherence to the prevailing *zeitgeist* keeps teachers from the essential work they must do; they stagnate, grow first uneasy, then frustrated and despondent. Soon, they leave the profession. There is nothing to do and nothing to be done. Czeslaw Milosz warns, "Because he who does not constantly overcome himself—i.e. does not learn and does not act—disintegrates within . . ." (2002, 273). But today there is little opportunity for the teacher to grow in the restrictive and constricting environment of public education. It is no wonder that the teacher leaves school exhausted at the end of each day. It is not just with standards and mandated curricula and administrators and students that a teacher must grapple: it is with herself she must struggle. Milosz argues that the artist and the revolutionary are alike: no one puts words on paper or paints on canvas doubting what they do or without acting according to their beliefs. Today, few consider teachers as anything but technocrats and poorly prepared lackeys. But it might be that teachers could be known as artists and revolutionaries: to be a teacher means to possess beliefs on which to act and to have the courage to act upon those beliefs. To take such a stance today and each day enacts a quiet and mostly invisible heroism that seems to go against the very nature of the American psyche. Perhaps though not supermen, teachers might begin to think of themselves as revolutionaries and artists: heroes.

Sometimes—alas, rarely—in the texts I study there appear exemplary models of such teachers. These teacher-heroes know either from the outset that, despite the public rhetoric, eating even the first frog will not be good for their health and they refuse to swallow it even if others reluctantly accept whatever is placed on their plate. Or there are those teachers whose stomachs turn at the third frog and who cannot swallow it. These heroes suffer the insecurities of their own private doubts about what meaning their work actually enjoys; these heroes suffer existential dread in their role as the ones who know even when their knowledge denies them this comfort; and they suffer the edicts and forced compromises that emanate from what Milosz refers to as the Center, though these teachers recognize these directives as antithetical to the work they know they must do. Every day they stand before their students vulnerable but responsible, and sometimes even achieve a success of which they might remain unaware and for which they certainly receive little acknowledgment. And sometimes all of their effort realizes little success. They are heroes.

One such exemplar is Murray Ringold in Philip Roth's novel *I Married a Communist.* Though the titular hero of the book is Ira Ringold, the actual communist, it is Ira's brother, Murray—Nathan Zuckerman's high school English teacher, whose conversations with Zuckerman over six long summer evenings comprise the narrative substance of the book—who seems to me to be the actual hero of the book. Murray's efforts as a teacher address directly Vladimir's question—what should we do?—even as it exemplifies the Rabbi's urgings that what we must do while waiting for whomever it is we are to await is to study and do acts of benevolence. The novel's narrative serves as the teacher's last lesson. As Murray's first lessons prepared Zuckerman for his life as a writer, Murray's last lesson as teacher will cast a shadow over Zuckerman's engagements in life.

The Zuckerman texts in Roth's corpus—narratives that chronicle and explain (in part) Zuckerman's withdrawal from an active to a hermetic life—offer evidence of the success *and* the failure of Murray's teaching. In contrast to the reclusive Zuckerman, Murray Ringold had remained engaged with and committed to his life in the school despite the public disdain he endured as a teacher, considered at the time a woman's profession, and the political difficulties he suffered as a teacher for his work with the union in its struggles to improve the status of the teaching profession. Murray's union activities were intended to combat "the personal indignity that you had to undergo as a teacher . . . [to be] treated like children" (Roth 1998, 5) and had identified him with the Communist left (to which he did not, in fact, belong) but which association led eventually to his dismissal during the worst days of the McCarthy era persecutions. To support his family Murray sold vacuum cleaners door-to-door. Six years of court struggle earned him back the teaching position that he did not again leave until his late retirement. And despite the difficulty of the work intrinsic to the teaching profession, Murray Ringold expressed no doubt concerning the social and personal significance of his position as teacher and learner.

Murray's ethical and intellectual commitment to the profession came, however, at great personal cost and professional difficulty. After a court order demanding his reinstatement, Murray spent the rest of his career in the Newark city public school system. Even as the social conditions in the city deteriorated, Murray refused to abandon either his school or riot-torn Newark despite the urgings of his colleagues who had long-migrated to the schools in the mostly white, middle-class suburbs. Twice mugged, Murray refused to flee what he understood as his moral responsibility. Ultimately, Doris, his wife, was murdered in the streets on her walk home from work when a mugger demanded her handbag that had, in fact, no money in it. Murray summarizes his life to Zuckerman: I was, he says, "[h]ad by myself, in case you're wondering. Myself with all my principles. I can't betray my brother. I can't betray my teaching, I can't betray the disadvantaged of Newark. . . . Doris paid the price of my civic virtue" (317). Having lost all of his illusions, all that endured was the *myth* of his own goodness, and though that goodness was admirable, he had come to accept that whatever might have been his intentions—his goodness—the myth of his goodness smashed upon the reality of the world. This acknowledgment exists as part of the teacher's last lesson: I can't do this all on my own; no, I'm no superman. Unlike Zuckerman, who admitted that in his life "I had chucked everything with which I no longer wish to contend, everything but what was need to live on and to work with" (321), Murray remained committed to his ethics despite his inability to effect much by them. "I spent the last ten years there, until I retired. Couldn't teach anybody anything. Barely able to hold down the mayhem, let alone teach . . . But how could I run away? I was interested in respect being shown for these kids" (316–17). Unlike Zuckerman, Murray remains committed to an activist life despite the lack of evidence of any results. It is not that Zuckerman has not learned from his teacher; rather, it is that he rejected the lesson. When Murray asks Zuckerman "What are you warding off? What the hell happened?" Zuckerman responds, "I listened carefully to your story, that's what happened" (320). As we teachers well know, lessons may even be learned and still not practiced, or they may be practiced but not in ways we originally intended.

Murray is the novel's hero because though he often stumbles, he always struggles to raise himself up, and in that struggle to help others accomplish the same. Zuckerman says,

> All the while I was listening to Murray—and looking at the needle of a man he's become and thinking of his physique as the materialization of all that coherence of his, as the consequence of a lifelong indifference to everything other than liberty in its most austere sense . . . thinking that Murray was an essentialist, that his character wasn't contingent, that wherever he'd found himself, even selling vacuum cleaners, he's managed to find his dignity . . . thinking that Murray (whom I didn't love or have to; with whom there was just the contract, teacher and student) was Ira (whom I did love) in a more mental, sensible, matter-of-fact version, Ira with a practical, clear, well-defined social goal, Ira without the heroically exaggerated ambitions, without that passionate overheated relationship to everything, Ira unblurred by impulse and the argument with everything . . . (16).

Invisible as he has been rendered by the society and at times by even his students, Murray nevertheless challenged his students daily with the courage of the revolutionary, the confidence of the artist: he epitomizes the teacher as hero.

Murray Ringold had come home from service in World War II and *chosen* to become a high school English teacher. To Murray, teaching was more than important: teaching was essential. "If there's any chance for the improvement of life," Murray explains to Zuckerman, in language that echoes the teachings of John Dewey and George Counts, "where's it going to begin if not in the school?" (317). Forty-seven years after the adolescent Zuckerman had sat in Murray's classroom, Zuckerman again sits in Ringold's classroom, in thrall at the mastery and wisdom of the teacher. Sitting on the porch of the cloistered home in Western Massachusetts to which Zuckerman has retreated from the life the teacher has refused to abandon, over six summer evenings Murray narrates to Zuckerman Ira Ringold's troubled life and Murray's engagement in it during a disturbing era in American history now referred to as the McCarthy Era. Murray even offers his student, Nathan Zuckerman, autobiographical insight on the trajectory of his own life: a fellowship application that had been rejected because of his association with the Ringold brothers, Murray and Ira. This understanding becomes part of the last lesson that Zuckerman acknowledges about our lives: there is so much about them we do not know! "Of course, it should not be too surprising to find out that your life story has included an event, something important, that you have known nothing about—your life story is in and of itself something that you know very little about" (15). Perhaps few have the opportunity to understand their lives narratively and do not therefore examine it for effects and causes, tropes and themes, though this *might be* the work of our classrooms—but it is in the last lesson from his teacher that Zuckerman comes to some resigned understanding of his own life.

This process, I suppose, represents a classic example of *currere,* and perhaps that ought to be the subject of another essay. Nevertheless, Murray's narration is a passionate and riveting story;

its themes serve for Zuckerman as his teacher's last lesson. In several months Murray, at the age of ninety, will have died. At this last meeting of teacher and student, Murray commands Zuckerman to do something with Ira's story. The novel *I Married a Communist* is the product of this last lesson, and it is the story of a hero, though it is not Ira but Murray who achieves this eminence.

From the beginning, Zuckerman understood in Murray's commitment a dedication to a moral code that his teaching epitomized. "You felt, in the sexual sense, the power of a male high school teacher like Murray Ringold—masculine authority uncorrected by piety—and you felt, *in the priestly sense,* the vocation of a male high school teacher who wasn't lost in the amorphous American aspiration to make it big, who—unlike the school's women teachers—could have chosen to be almost anything else and chose instead, for his life work, to be ours. All he wanted all day long was to deal with young people he could influence, and his biggest kick in life he got from their response" (italics added, 2). *In the priestly sense,* the teacher supported and nurtured the spirit of his students, acted with responsibility and concern for what could only be described as their spiritual development. "I burned with zeal to establish the dignity of my profession . . . I was interested in respect being shown for these kids." For Murray, teaching was an ethical, even a prophetic calling, and he had committed his life to the profession. "I was a professional schoolteacher, reading books, teaching Shakespeare, making you kids diagram sentences and memorize poetry and appreciate literature. I thought no other life worth living." Zuckerman says, "Teaching was a passionate occupation for him, and he was an exciting guy" (77). Like the priest, Murray had committed his life to the care of others and the betterment of society.

Ringold had been Zuckerman's first English teacher and, noting Zuckerman's output, apparently one of the great influences on his life, though at the time this was not obvious to the young

Zuckerman. "Not that the impression his bold classroom style left on my sense of freedom was apparent at the time: no kid thought that way about school or teachers or himself" (2). As a teacher Murray provided his students with the model and the method for intellectual engagement, not simply by the content he taught but by the stance he assumed in the classroom. Zuckerman says, "Mr. Ringold brought with him into the classroom a charge of visceral spontaneity that was a revelation to tamed, respectablized kids who were yet to comprehend that obeying a teacher's rules of decorum had nothing to do with mental development. . . . His special talent was for dramatizing inquiry, for casting a strong narrative spell even when he was being strictly analytic and scrutinizing aloud, in his clear-cut way, what we read and wrote" (2). Zuckerman describes not merely this novel's method but that of all the Zuckerman books in the Roth corpus: analysis, intellectual scrutiny, and philosophical speculation concerning life's meaning: what is it all about, Alfie? Ringold's pedagogy was about method rather than content. "'In human society,' Mr. Ringold taught us, 'thinking's the greatest transgression of all. Cri-ti-cal think-ing,' Mr. Ringold said, using his knuckles to rap out each of the syllables on his desktop, '—there is the ultimate subversion'" (2). And Zuckerman adds, "I told Murray that hearing this early on from a manly guy like him—seeing it demonstrated by him—provided the most valuable clue to growing up that I had clutched at, albeit half comprehendingly, as a provincial, protected, high-minded high school kid yearning to be rational and of consequence and free." In this last lesson, Zuckerman confesses that he had learned that lesson wisely and too well.

Almost one hundred years earlier, William James (1892/1961, 320) had expressed an idea similar to Murray's. James had written, "*To sustain a representation, to think,* is in short, the only moral act, for the impulsive, and the obstructed, for sane and lunatics alike . . . not only our morality but our religion, so far as the latter is deliberate, depend on the effort we can make. *Will you or won't you have it so.*" In *his* talk to teachers (94–5) James urges them: "See to it now . . . that you make freemen of your pupils by habituating them to act, whenever possible, under the notion of a good. Get them habitually to tell the truth, not so much through showing them the wickedness of lying as by arousing their enthusiasm for honesty and veracity. Wean them from their native cruelty by imparting to them some of your own positive sympathy with an animal's inner springs of joy." I think James' urging to the teachers is enacted in Murray Ringold's teaching. "You know," he says to Zuckerman, "I was a professional, a schoolteacher, reading books, teaching Shakespeare, making you kids diagram sentences and memorize poetry and appreciate literature, and I thought no other kind of life was worth living" (Roth, 1998, 134). And Murray's last lesson will help Zuckerman *and the reader* understand the motives for Zuckerman's failure. Paradoxically, Zuckerman's success as a novelist derives in part from his English teacher, Murray Ringold, even as Zuckerman's acknowledgment of his social failure derives in part from Murray's last lesson.

Murray's emphasis on critical thinking serves not to discover the answer but to commit to the question. It was in town and down the road from the home to which he had retreated from the world that Zuckerman again comes upon Murray Ringold, who at the age of ninety had enrolled at an elder hostel at Athena College. One night, after Zuckerman had picked Murray up for their evening get-together on Zuckerman's front porch, he notes that Murray had been writing a short assigned paper. Murray was still learning. Zuckerman comments, "I shouldn't have been surprised at his mental energy, even by his enthusiasm for the three-hundred-word writing assignment . . . that the professor had given his elderly students. Yet that a man so close to oblivion should be preparing homework for the next day, educating himself for a life that had all but run out—that the puzzle continued to puzzle him, that clarification remained a vital need—more than surprised me . . ." (151). The ultimate teacher, Murray even at ninety years of age continues to seek out an answer to his question. Nathan Zuckerman had long retired from that quest.

As Murray narrates the story of his brother Ira Ringold, he portrays life as the unfathomable intricacy of human motive and action that people attempt to simplify, categorize, and dismiss, even as in the schools today education is reduced to the results on standardized tests and prescribed curricula. At least, this is what Murray's story about Ira comes to mean to Nathan Zuckerman, Murray's student. What is it all about, Alfie? Murray's last lesson suggests to Zuckerman that nobody really knows what it is all about. Murray confesses to Zuckerman that Eve Frame, his brother Ira's wife who had published the ghost-written exposé entitled *I Married a Communist*, didn't really marry a communist because to assign him this label would have been to reduce the complexity of human life to a lie. Rather, Murray says, Eve married a man hungering after a life, but a man who could not construct one into which he could fit. And having heard this story in which Zuckerman played a central role—though not until this last lesson does he become wholly aware of how his life had been shaped by those early events—Zuckerman says to Ringold, as if talking to the teacher, "It's all error . . . Isn't that what you've been telling me? There's only error. *There's* the heart of the world. Nobody finds his life. That *is* life." Murray, his English teacher, now ninety years old and only several months from his death, has offered one last lesson about life to his illustrious student.

It is clear to me (a teacher) that Roth has designated Murray, the teacher, as the hero of this novel because it was Murray, the teacher, who had remained committed to life in his teaching. Despite the implications of this last lesson, Murray had continued to keep on keeping on. Murray's commitment to his teaching saved neither his students, nor Newark, nor himself because in this life there is no connection between intention and result. "What's it all about, Alfie?" Roth's Zuckerman responds that he has learned that "It's all about nothing." It is what Vladimir and

Estragon state at the play's opening: "Nothing to be done." But Murray Ringold, the teacher, suggests that life is not about nothing though sometimes nothing might be its apparent yield. Rather, the teacher had committed himself to assist the helpless Pozzo *here* and *now* because the here and now is all he can ultimately control. And it is Murray's presence in this book as a teacher that offers Zuckerman this last lesson even though his now-famous student will not act on what he has learned. Down here, where everything matters, it can *seem* that it isn't about anything: in response to this uncertainty Zuckerman has run away from life. "I had chucked everything with which I no longer wish to contend, everything but what was needed to live on and to work with. I set out to receive all my fullness from what might once have seemed, even to me, not nearly enough and to inhabit passionately only the parts of speech" (321). Zuckerman had retreated from life only to write in his books about that failure. He is not his own hero: at first almost embarrassed by Murray's continued pursuit of the question, Zuckerman soon retreats back into his reserve: "But then the sense of error vanished. There were no more difficulties I wished to create." Unlike his teacher who had never ceased to search out the complexity that the question demanded, Zuckerman had given up.

And despite Zuckerman's resistance, Murray's last lesson as a teacher continues to have effect. Zuckerman says,

> We could have sat on my deck for six hundred nights before I heard the entire story of how Murray Ringold, who'd chosen to be nothing more extraordinary than a high school teacher, had failed to elude the turmoil of this time and place and ended up no less a historical casualty than his brother. This was the existence that America had worked out for him—and that he'd worked out for himself by thinking, by taking his revenge on his father by cri-ti-cal think-ing, by being reasonable in the face of no reason . . . This was what adhering to his convictions had got him, resisting the

tyranny of compromise. If there's any chance for the improvement of life, where's it going to begin if not in the school? Hopelessly entangled in the best of intentions, tangibly, over a lifetime, committed to a constructive course that is not an illusion, to formulations and solutions that will no longer wash (318).

It is only the intentions that Murray could control and not their consequences over which he had none that derives Murray's dignity and heroism.

It is this realization that constitutes part of the teacher's last lesson: one's intentions may be admirable but they do not govern events. Murray's story teaches Zuckerman that "You control betrayal on one side and you wind up betraying somewhere else. Because it's not a static system. Because it's alive. Because everything that lives is in movement. Because purity is petrification. Because purity is a lie . . . you're urged on by five hundred things. Because without the pole of righteousness . . . without the big lie of righteousness to tell you why you do what you do, you have to ask yourself, along the way, 'Why *do* I do what I do?' And you have to endure yourself without knowing" (318). How do we become who we are? How do we choose our life paths? We have to endure without knowing. As teachers, in the classroom we act but we cannot know the ends of our actions. Nobody knows. "And you have to endure yourself without knowing." This stance constitutes the heroic nature of the teacher. But what test anywhere would measure this knowledge? But what learning might be more valuable?

At the end of "My Pedagogic Creed," John Dewey writes (in a language that Murray Ringold will echo almost one hundred years later): "Every teacher should realize the dignity of his calling; that he is a social servant set apart for the maintenance of proper social order and the securing of the right social growth; in this way the teacher always is the prophet of the true God and the usherer in of the true kingdom of God." The statement surprises many who have early learned to keep separate the secular from the sacred, and Dewey's assertion shocks many who see the teacher not as a social servant set apart but as a social servant meant to do the bidding of others and preferably that of the power-elite of the present social order. But for Dewey that proper social order is not that of the present structure of power but that which derives from democracy. Dewey here secularizes the sacred and makes the sacred secular. For Dewey, religion was an expression of the social relations of the community, and as Robert Westbrook (1991, 78–9) suggests, for Dewey "the kingdom of God on earth was an industrial democracy," and the prophet would be "the man who succeeds in pointing out the religious meaning of democracy." That meaning, as Dewey seems to have known even early in his professional life, rests on the idea that democracy enables us to get "truths in a natural, every-day and practical sense which otherwise could be grasped only in a somewhat unnatural or sentimental sense" (Dewey, 1893, 8). Thus, truths are arrived at in action. For Dewey the incipient pragmatist, truth is not what one possesses but that upon which one acts. As Murray Ringold would discover, the ends are often unknown, but the intentions are significant. Dewey says, "Democracy is freedom. If truth is at the bottom of things, freedom means giving this truth a chance to show itself, a chance to well up from the depths. Democracy, as freedom, means the loosening of bonds, the wearing away of restrictions, the breaking down of barriers, of middle walls, of partitions. Through this elimination of restrictions, whatever truth, whatever reality there is in man's life, is freed to express itself" (8). Knowledge is a tool by which truth can be freed, and democracy cannot exist if there be any restriction on knowledge that would prevent this freeing of truth. Democracy is then, revelation, and revelation is not a monopolistic possession of truth but a continuing process "as long as life has new meanings to unfold, new action to propose" (5). For Dewey, it is the teacher-as-prophet who calls out the demands of social justice upon which democracy insists in order that revelation be ongoing! I think that Murray Ringold's advocacy of "Cri-ti-cal think-ing, the ultimate subversion," exemplifies Dewey's ideal.

Teaching, as is prophecy, is an impossible profession. It pleases no one, least of all the prophet. What Heschel (1962, 9) says about the prophet holds equally true for the teacher: they are not like the others to whom "the moral state of society, for all its stains and spots, seems fair and trim; to the prophet it is dreadful." For the others, "So many deeds of charity are done, so much decency radiates day and night . . . standards are modest; our sense of injustice tolerable, timid; our moral indignation impermanent . . . To us life is often serene . . ." But, says Heschel, "in the prophet's eye the world reels in confusion. The prophet makes no concession to man's capacity. Exhibiting little understanding for human weakness, [the prophet] seems unable to extenuate the culpability of man." The teacher's role is to enable the students to engage in "the process of coming to share in the social consciousness," and to act as the one who knows that "the adjustment of individual activity on the basis of this social consciousness is the only sure method of social reconstruction" (Dewey, 1893, 437). The work is heroically hard. Spinoza taught and Murray Ringold enacts that understanding is a never-ending process. Spinoza writes (1955, 271), "If the way which I have pointed out as leading to this result seems exceedingly hard, it may nevertheless be discovered. Needs must it be hard, since it is so seldom found. How would it be possible, if salvation were ready to our hand, and could without great labour be found, that it should be by almost all men neglected? But all things excellent are as difficult as they are rare." "To be a prophet," Heschel (1962, 18) tells us, "means to challenge and to defy and to cast out fear." As Murray Ringold says, "If there's any chance for the improvement of life, where's it going to begin if not in the school?"

Not superman but prophet. Not martyr, but hero. The teacher. There exists for me still another exemplary portrayal of the teacher-hero in John Updike's 1963 novel, *The Centaur*. George Caldwell, a science teacher at Olinger High School, epitomizes for me the impossible paradox the teacher confronts: suffering his existential crisis, Caldwell doubts the foundation of his undertaking and, unlike Murray Ringold, questions if what he does has any purpose. Nevertheless, Caldwell continues daily to stand before a class of students advocating the very knowledge for which he experiences not simply distrust but fear. If the central curriculum question concerns what knowledge is of most worth, and our modern educational system epitomizes the question "whose knowledge is of most worth," then George Caldwell in *The Centaur* wonders how knowledge is of worth at all. What *is* it all about, Alfie? Caldwell's uncertainty sickens him because it seems to suggest that life leads only to death, the final meaninglessness. Caldwell's father had been a minister—a man whose life had been organized by faith—and on his deathbed had asked, "Will I be eternally forgotten?" Caldwell says, "That was a terrible thing for a minister to say. It scared the living daylights out of me" (73). I believe that what scared Caldwell was the idea that if one loses faith then to account for one's life may be a meaningless enterprise. By becoming a teacher, George had transferred his father's faith in God to a faith in knowledge, but at this moment that faith has failed him.

George searches desperately for some certainty to replace the doubt that underlies his practice. At the source of Caldwell's work in the class is his gnawing hesitation about purpose and meaning in the universe. Caldwell says, "I wouldn't mind plugging ahead at something I wasn't any good at if I knew what the hell the point of it all was. I ask, and nobody'll tell me." From everyone he meets he seeks some answer, but none seems forthcoming. His is not a problem about content, or methods, or even standards; what plagues Caldwell is existential angst about meaning, and what drives him in every moment is his quest to relieve that anxiety.

George struggles not with the classical question of curriculum: what knowledge is of most worth, but with the larger existential question: what value is knowledge at all if finally all knowledge leads to and is a record of death. For the minister, time should have been comfortingly eternal, but George understands that his father's doubts disturbed the foundations on which his life had been based. Now, the son and teacher, mystified and terrified by the eternality of time—he asks, Time and tide wait for no man ... Caldwell seeks some comfort in knowledge for his fear. But all of his knowledge seems to lead him to death, for which his knowledge has not prepared him. "I'm not ready and it scares the hell out of me. What's the answer?" (168), he asks his colleague. Death calls all of life into question, and for Caldwell—what is it all about Alfie?—all his knowledge seems to be about death, and he doubts the efficacy of his knowledge.

Everything about his subject matter reminds him of pain and loss. Caldwell, the science teacher, steps back from the chalkboard on which he has written the weight of the earth (6,000,000, 000,000,000,000,000 tons) and the weight of the sun (1,998,00 0,000,000,000,000,000,000 tons), and "looks at the numbers he has written, and shudders in fear . . . The zeros stared back, every one a wound leaking the word 'poison'"(33). "They remind me of death," Caldwell states, even as do the blank faces of his students. During this particular class, Caldwell has attempted to reduce the frightening sequence of the five billion years (5,000,000,000) of the earth's formation down to human dimension and, perhaps, human comprehension. He has for the purpose of this lesson condensed these impenetrable death-meaning eons to a span of a mere three days.[2] As the seconds of the class tick away, Caldwell desperately attempts to bring this story of creation to its climactic and even human moment, but no one seems at all attentive. "The first bell rang. The monitors stampeded out of the class . . . two boys bumped in the doorway and, thrashing, stabbed each other with pencils . . . a handful of BBs was flung into [Caldwell's] face" (39). But with his "very blood loathing the story he told" (40), Caldwell continues irrepressibly on with the lesson. Standing upright, Caldwell narrates the appearance of the human being in his narrative of evolution: "One minute ago flint-chipping, fire-kindling, death-foreseeing, a tragic animal appeared—called Man" (46). However, his glorious though apocryphally dramatic portrayal of the origin of the ultimately tragic, death-doomed human creature in this final and glorious moment of creation is missed in the deafening rumble that marks the riotous exit at the end of class. At the front of the room, Caldwell, the exasperated and defeated teacher, desperately tries to bring to a close his science lesson. "'Two minutes left,' Caldwell shouted. His voice had grown higher in pitch, as if a peg in his head were being turned. 'Keep your seats'" (39), he implores. Caldwell's entire presentation appears to him to have failed completely.

This pursuit of meaning underlies not only his role in the classroom, but serves also to organize his entire stance in life. His son, Peter, writes, "My father brought to conversations a cavernous capacity for caring that dismayed strangers. They found themselves, willy-nilly, in a futile but urgent search for the truth" (66). To the hitchhiker George says, "Most dogs won't hurt you . . . They're just like I am, curious" (70). And to the drunk on the street who accuses George of being a child molester and yet to whom he gives his last thirty-five cents, George says, "I've enjoyed talking to you . . . and I'd like to shake your hand . . . You've clarified my thinking" (122). Later, at the high school basketball game, ever seeking answers, Caldwell confronts the Reverend March with his religious doubts, but Caldwell only manages to anger and embarrass the minister with his questions. Caldwell had been wondering about what he perceived as the injustice of God's division of all humankind into the categories of the elect and the non-elect. He wonders how God could be considered merciful if this same God created those who would never "get it" and therefore, would be never saved, those like his students, or even George himself. Caldwell sees no justice in this distinction; the entire scheme appears cruel and vindictive. There is no meaning to life save for the few elect. "The only reason I could figure out was that God had to have somebody to fry down in Hell" (189). The same condition applies in the school and with the students who might never "get it," like Judy Lengel, and who, therefore would never be saved. Of what purpose could the teacher be to these unfortunates, Caldwell considers. Of what value is knowledge to them? But the minister, exasperated, perhaps even a little embarrassed by Caldwell's questions, and at the same time lasciviously attentive to the girls' gym teacher, Vera Hummel, dismisses Caldwell and his doubts, and suggests that he really ought to make an appointment to continue the discussion at some future time in the minister's office. Religion offers neither relief from Caldwell's doubts nor strength to shore up his fragile faith. Nevertheless, daily, Caldwell returns to his classroom successfully, albeit unbeknownst to him, to confront alone these primary doubts. Caldwell's obituary notes, "What endures, perhaps, most indelibly in the minds of his ex-students (of whom this present writer counts himself one) was his more-than-human selflessness, a total concern for the world at large which left him, perhaps, too little margin for self-indulgence and satisfied repose. To sit under Mr. Caldwell was to lift up one's head in aspiration." Ironically, here it is not his work but his role as a teacher that stands out: the prophet of the one true God.

"It's no Golden Age, that's for sure," says George Caldwell, our modern day Chiron. During that mythological Golden Age, Chiron, the noblest centaur, taught the children of the gods—Jason, Achilles, Asclepios, his own daughter, Ocyrhoe, and the dozen other princely children of Olympus abandoned to his care. There, in that bucolic classroom the subject was "Love," which Chiron says, "set the Universe in motion." The teacher continued: "All things that exist are her children—sun, moon, stars, the earth with the mountains and rivers, its trees, herbs, and living creatures" (78).

THE LAST LESSON

There, in that pastoral site during that Golden Age, the teacher, Chiron, walked "a little late, down the corridors of tamarisk, yew, bay and kermes oak. Beneath the cedars and silver firs, whose hushed heads were shadows permeated with Olympian blue, a vigorous underwood of arbutus, wild pear, cornel, box and andrachne filled with scents of flower and sap and new twig the middle air of the forest" (74). Chiron's classroom is paradisiacal, his students bright and eager, and the teacher made whole in his pedagogical encounters: "[Chiron's] students," Updike writes, "completed the Centaur." Chiron's is a classroom filled with light, warmth and meaning; images of circles abound everywhere in that idyllic classroom.

But this time in which we live is no Golden Age. "Love's scepter has passed to Uranus . . ." who, it is said, arrives under the cover of the starless night sky to copulate with his mother, Gaia. It is in this world dominated by darkness and dubious moral balance that Chiron's contemporary counterpart, George Caldwell, functions; it is this darkness that obscures the meaning of which Chiron was so certain, but of which Caldwell despairingly doubts yet for which he desperately seeks. Caldwell epitomizes the ironies of knowing. Though he knows something, his knowledge sickens him because he sees no value in it. To his wife's plaint "It must be terrible to know so much," Caldwell answers, "It is . . . It's hell" (217). Ironically, however, it is impossible for the teacher Caldwell (and what else is a teacher but a learner grown old, Doc Appleton asks Caldwell) to cease to want to know, to cease to search for a certain knowledge but to acknowledge its ephemerality, and to offer to provide to others something of what he might have learned, even if this task is impossibly hard, seemingly ineffectual, and leads him knowingly and inevitably toward death. If Chiron's students complete him, Caldwell's students tear him apart. In this modern classroom, a tenuous truce is all that Caldwell desires: "I don't *want* you to like me," Caldwell exclaims resignedly. "All I want from you is to sit still under me for fifty-five minutes a day five days a week" (81). And if in Chiron's bucolic class the polyphony of voices formed a rainbow, in Caldwell's room the cacophony of sound produces only storm.

This is no Golden Age. If nothing more, these schoolrooms are very much of the earth. They smell of sweat and over-the-counter scents, of bad breath and flatulence, of coffees and stale foods, of chalk and dry erase markers. The air that pervades them is too often too visible, filled with motes of stale dust floating under the ubiquitous fluorescent lighting and hovering over the disappointment of containment. The high piercing voices of young children strike through this air like sudden cracklings of lightning, filling the spaces with uncontainable energy but barely usable illumination. Their voices are like the gaggling of ducks or geese flying onto their next destination: they squawk in exuberance and purpose but seemingly unmindful to any need for response. In the schoolrooms of the older children, a frustrated pandemonium reigns fueled by frustration, boredom, and hormones.

These places seethe with the immanent potency and danger of colliding tectonic plates. In the halls echoes whisper, and in the classrooms the steadfast, steady sound of the teacher's commanding voice seasoned with despairing notes of warning pins students to their seats with questions and imprecations, demands and disapprovals. In these classrooms a palpable tension charges the air, arising out of the antagonism between the quiet of responses that is as close to silence as silence and the terror of notice that causes others to look intently through their desks to the floor below, a tension borne out of the clash of conflicting desires and seething resentments. Crumbled paper and pencil shavings, candy wrappers, and sheets ripped out of notebooks litter the surface; gum and snot coat the underside of chairs and desks. Everyone knows—because they have been contributors to such detritus—not to reach under except to add to the array; even custodians avoid this onerous task until year's end. The desks and chairs, sometimes rooted and sometimes free standing, held in place only by the severity of the teacher's compulsion, scrape and grate painfully on the floors; tipped back chairs fall heavily backwards to the alarm of the one seated and the delight of everyone else but the terrified, exasperated teacher who foresaw this event and stood powerless to prevent it. Shoes chafe noisily on the floors. Atop the desk tops books, papers, and pens are arrayed, beneath which are concealed signs written and carved for rebellious purpose and signs of more honest presence: *I♥Paul; Mr. Billings is a dork; π=450 calories. Fuck everyone!* In the science rooms the pungent odors of sulfur dioxide and formaldehyde hang aloft oppressively, and then ooze out of the doorways to mix obscenely in the halls with the unappetizing aromas of food preparation emanating from cafeteria kitchens. The unsavory smells hang suspended in the air, and then settle, like ice-nine, on everything, threatening to freeze all movement. In sum, the mingling of odors produces a potent dankness particular only to schools, places of worship, and mortuary crypts, such as that where Romeo and Juliet ended their brief lives.

It is here that Caldwell spends his days and sometimes evenings. (I have measured my life, too, in these rooms. When I am there, as Bartleby said in the Tombs, I know where I am. I am a teacher, and even if I were not so, I have known teachers. This is no Golden Age, though gold here exists.)

The Centaur portrays poignantly the anguish and triumph of George Caldwell, the teacher, struggling to discover and to communicate some order and meaning in life, but whose purposes seem forever frustrated by his own doubts and by the world in which he functions. Overwhelmed at times by the nature of his task, Caldwell confesses to Hester Appleton, the language teacher at Olinger High School, "There've been times in my years here when the kids have got me so down I've stepped out of the classroom and come here by the drinking fountain just to hear you in there pronouncing French . . ." (147). I think what Caldwell sought outside that classroom was solidity, certainty, beauty, even faith, but all around him he seems to confront doubt, ambiguity, ugliness, and spite, his own classroom a scene of tension, conflict, and frustration. There, in that space assigned to learning, menace, chaos, dissatisfaction, and failure seem to reign. There, in that classroom, "Fists, claws, cocked elbows blurred in patch-colored panic above the scarred and varnished desk-tops . . ." (42). Though the centaur Chiron's students, "Hail him gladly" (75), the first sentence of *The Centaur* narrates that as George Caldwell moved toward the chalkboard he "turned and as he turned his ankle received an arrow. The class burst into laughter" (9). The pain opened in his body like a spider, but from his pain Caldwell finds relief nowhere in the school; indeed, even "his fellow teachers seemed herdsmen of terror, threatening to squeeze him back into the room with his students" (10). To Caldwell all seems useless and hopeless; and yet, though this is no Golden Age, though Caldwell's efforts seem to bear no fruit, and though his classroom appears to him a scene of dissonance, suspicion, and antagonism, though he doubts his capacity to effect any purpose, almost beyond his ken, this contemporary Chiron, George Caldwell, succeeds exactly because his humility and existential doubt inspire a sympathy with his adolescent charges that surpasses in effect the subject matter content he must communicate.

His, however, is a futile struggle. Resigned to almost inevitable disappointment and defeat, Caldwell acknowledges: "[T]he one thing you learn in teaching; people forget everything you tell 'em. I look at those dumb blank faces every day and it reminds me of death. You fall through those kids' heads without a trace" (73). Caldwell's purpose seems to him hopeless, and his sense of his own meaninglessness oppresses him. "After every weekend," his son, Peter, writes, "my father had to gather his nerve to go back to teaching" (41). But return to the school is what Caldwell always does: ironically, it is where he feels most at home. Because he is a seeker, Caldwell paradoxically feels competent and purposeful only in the school, though it is in school that he despairs of his efficacy. Ironically, Caldwell is comfortable only in school where, he perceptively and ironically quips, "the monsters are ready to learn," but where, in his efforts, he nevertheless confronts their resistance and his own inevitable doubt and angst blinding him to its worth.

Caldwell repeatedly bemoans the apparent ineffectiveness of his efforts, and confesses his doubts of the efficacy of his effort. He concedes his powerlessness, incompetence, and irrelevance with a certain irony and regret. Preparing to leave for school, Caldwell announces to his father-in-law, Pop Kramer, "I love lies, I tell 'em all day. I'm paid to tell them" (42). And when, at the end of class, Judy Lengel asks Caldwell for some advance notice about information that will be on the upcoming quiz, information that he tells her he can't honestly give, she cries, "I get so sort of sick and dizzy just trying to keep it straight." Caldwell admits, "We *all* do . . . Knowledge is a sickening thing" (85). Caldwell's despair derives from the burden of an overwhelming existential doubt to which his experience and knowledge have led him and from which he cannot seem to escape. Unlike Chiron, his mythological counterpart, Caldwell does not believe that he has the capacity or the skill to bring these children out of darkness, not merely as a result of his perceived incompetence, but because there may be nothing out there but the presence of darkness. Nevertheless, Caldwell is constrained to keep on keeping on. Puzzled by the word *book* carved into the walls above the urinal in the boy's bathroom, Caldwell suddenly understands that the original carving has been altered. "Willing to learn, even by the last flash of light before annihilation, he absorbs the fact totally new to him, that every FUCK could be made into a BOOK" (185). What else is a teacher but one who daily makes that effort to turn every FUCK into a BOOK, but remains painfully aware that there is no end to the FUCKS in the world. This is more than a pedagogical exercise; it is an ethical imperative.

And yet, Updike's modern Chiron succeeds despite his existential doubts and apprehensions. Indeed, the only one who doubts his value is Caldwell himself. Ironically, Caldwell's success as a teacher occurs beyond his knowledge. Despite his self-deprecation ("Christ," he moans, "the only place I can go if I leave this school is the junkyard. I'm no good for anything else. I never was.") Caldwell is, in fact, a wonderful teacher. "You've received no favors from me," Principal Zimmerman tells Caldwell. "You're a good teacher" (187). Updike's portrait of the teacher in this text speaks to the ideal nature of the troubled teacher in what is no longer a Golden Age. In the obituary written by his former student and nemesis, Diefendorf, Caldwell is described as having

> a thorough mastery of his subjects, an inexhaustible sympathy for the scholastic underdog, a unique ability to make unexpected connections and to mix in an always fresh and eye-opening way the stuff of lessons with the stuff of life, an effortless humor, a by no means negligible gift for dramatization, a restless and doubting temperament that urged him forward ceaselessly towards self-improvement in the pedagogic craft . . . To sit under Mr. Caldwell was to lift up one's head in aspiration . . . there was never any confusion that indeed 'Here was a man' (133).

Alas, Caldwell would have understood none of this encomium. As with all teachers, perhaps, their success occurs always in some unrevealed future and in a place beyond their knowledge. And the teachers' achievement occurs not as a result of the subject content they are able to transmit, but from the content of their character of which the mastery of subject content is only a single part. The teacher's success occurs in the absence of quantifiable measured results on some testing instrument. In the end, Diefendorf, Caldwell's impossible student, becomes a teacher because of his love and respect for his teacher, George Caldwell.

And yet, to Caldwell the school appears rife with animosity and hostility. Heading out with his son to school each morning, Caldwell cries out, only half-humorously, "Off to the slaughterhouse. Those damn kids have put their hate right into my bowels . . . Off to the hate factory" (49). He feels alienated and overcome in his work, and the futility of his effort overwhelms Caldwell with the sense of his absolute worthlessness. "[T]he Founding Fathers in their wisdom decided that children were an unnatural strain on parents. So they provided jails called schools, equipped with tortures called an education . . . I am a paid keeper of Society's unusables—the lame, the halt, the insane, and the ignorant" (80). At the school basketball game, plagued by his own doubt, Caldwell encounters his former students whom he imagines as the products of his failure: "Living corpses, they didn't even have the sense to stay out once they got out . . . What in hell are you supposed to do to keep them from ending like that" (188). These students make Caldwell anxious, representing as they do evidences of his inefficacy. "He shies away from these old students, the hunch in their shoulders reminding him of the great whole skinned carcasses hung on hooks in the freezer of a big Atlantic City hotel he once worked for" (188). Wherever he looks, Caldwell confronts death, failure, and meaninglessness, and he suffers painfully his inability to relieve either his dread or what he imagines as the despairing fate of his students.

And it is not merely those who cannot leave the school that causes Caldwell to experience defeat; even in those who have become active citizens does Caldwell assume the consequences of his failure as a teacher. Suffering from a toothache, Caldwell visits the dental office of one of his former students who proceeds to extract the tooth. "The kid had wanted to become an M.D. but hadn't the I.Q. so he had settled on being a butcher. Caldwell recognizes the pain branching in his head as a consequence of some failing in his own teaching, a failure somewhere to inculcate in this struggling soul consideration and patience; and accepts it as such" (164). Caldwell's frustrations confront him everywhere; his seems an irrelevant existence. To his son, Peter, he says, "The only incentive I can give you, kid, to behave yourself is this: if you don't buckle down and learn something, you'll be as dumb as

I am, and you'll have to teach school to earn a living" (102). This is no Golden Age, though there is gold to be found. Updike portrays Caldwell as a forsaken saint in this modern tarnished world. To his self-deprecatory statement, "I'm a dime a dozen," Peter says to his father, almost exasperatedly but really in admiration, "But there's nobody else like you, Daddy. There's nobody else like you in the world" (194). But his father does not hear. This self-sacrificing, questing teacher, functioning seemingly without effect and purpose, but whose character and efficacy are unquestioned by the novel, is nevertheless the hero in this novel. *The Centaur* offers the teacher as modern guardian of knowledge and moral virtue. It is the example of this teacher's effort that will bring the children out of darkness.

It is exactly from his seemingly selfless, endlessly searching stance as a teacher that Caldwell's suffering and his success derives: his life seems committed and sustained by responsibility to others but without a grounding in belief in knowledge. He admits to the doctor's wife, Hester Appleton, "I can't afford to die" (146), to which she answers, "It is a luxury." Caldwell remains bound by his obligations. Or rather, this sense of responsibility is his ethical stance before the Others he daily confronts. A teacher is all that Caldwell can be; teaching is all he must do. Though Caldwell's father had bequeathed to him a sense of doubt, rootlessness, and even despair, Caldwell is committed to provide for his son and his students some direction, and it is in the school, where knowledge occurs, that Caldwell is, oddly enough, most comfortable. "It's all I'm good for, Cassie," Caldwell says to his wife, "It's my one talent. I can't quit" (214). And though the world to him is an impenetrable mystery, he cannot cease seeking answers in it. Caldwell remains unfailingly committed to the struggle. As Doc Appleton, diagnosing Caldwell's physical complaints, says to him, "You're not a teacher, you're a learner. This creates tension" (101). That tension torments Caldwell and yet provides the foundation for his stance in the school. And ironically, though knowledge seems to be that for which he quests, and though he is a teacher, Caldwell doesn't evince too much faith in his search. "Ignorance is bliss," he says to his colleague, "That's the lesson I've gotten out of life" (169). It is an ironic comment from a man engaged in learning, ironic also because ignorance is the state out of which Caldwell desperately seeks to move.

In that ethical stance in which he commands others to command him, Caldwell compromises his own safety and security. Caldwell teaches that this sense of responsibility and mortality exists as an essential aspect of creation, not as a result of blind evolutionary development but by deliberate choice. During his lecture Caldwell attributes the reality of Death to the ethical volvox:

> There is no reason intrinsic in the plasmic substance why life should ever end. Amoebas never die . . . But the volvox, a rolling sphere of flagellating algae organized into somatic and reproductive cells . . . by pioneering this new idea of *cooperation*, rolled life into the kingdom of certain—as opposed to accidental—death. For—hold tight kids, just seven more minutes of torture—while each cell is potentially immortal by volunteering for a specialized function within an organized society of cells, it enters a compromised environment (37).

It is this same responsibility that leads Caldwell to sacrifice his life for others—his wife, Cassie; his father-in-law, Pop Kramer; his son, Peter; and the multitude of students who have sat under Caldwell in that science classroom—and which leads to the identification of him with the Centaur Chiron, who chose to die so that Prometheus could live, even as Jesus chose his death supposedly for the salvation of others. It might be Caldwell's ultimate identification with Chiron and the volvox that affords him peace and purpose. The teacher has served his god—the quest for answers—and he may die knowing the answer has been to try.

I think Updike has chosen the myth of the centaur Chiron in order to illustrate the sanctity of this teacher, George Caldwell.

In the final chapter of the novel, Updike conflates the death of the Centaur Chiron with that of the Teacher Caldwell. Updike writes: "The time left him possessed a skyey breadth in which he swam like a true grandchild of Oceanus; he discovered that in giving his life to others he entered a total freedom. Mt. Ide and Mt. Ditke from opposite blue distances rushed toward him like clapping waves and in the upright of his body Sky and Gaia mated again. Only goodness lives. But it does live" (220). Caldwell, the teacher, dies having offered his life so that others might live. I believe that it is this insight, this awareness that his life *has* had purpose, though that purpose remains unrealized and even unknown and even unknowable,[3] that finally allows Caldwell to accept death. At the novel's end, Caldwell comes to understand that, indeed, goodness lives, though in the schools that quality is not always evident.

Despite George Caldwell's personal and existential doubt, despite his acknowledgment that this is no Golden Age, and despite the disordered and earthly nature of his classroom, George Caldwell exemplifies the myth-like nature of the modern teacher. Updike means to raise the mundane to the level of the heavenly. In *The Centaur*, the teacher does not achieve divinity by his work, but does his work because he is divine. On Mount Olympus, the centaur Chiron served as teacher to the children of the gods, even as here on earth, George Caldwell, our modern day Chiron, teaches the children of Olinger's citizens. It is the intention of both to bring the children out of darkness, though it is only the former who has faith in his efforts. "Zeus loved his old friend, and lifted him up, and set him among the stars as the constellation Sagittarius. Here, in the Zodiac, now above, now below the horizon, he assists in the regulation of our destinies, though in this latter time few living morals cast their eyes respectfully toward Heaven, and few still sit as students to the stars" (222). In this Pennsylvania classroom that reeks of the earth, human beings do divine things because they are teachers, though few sit still as students.

This is no Golden Age, and faith is on the wane. But I would argue that despite the reality that this may be no Golden Age (if indeed, there ever was one), and despite Updike's skeptical, even cynical vision of a fallen world, in *The Centaur* Updike presents a world, perhaps desecrated, but not without hope of redemption nor even one absent of gold. In *The Centaur,* Updike portrays the teacher, George Caldwell, our contemporary Chiron, as the ethical guardian of that world in which knowledge has replaced faith as bulwark against chaos and moral decline. In this novel, it is the teacher who offers *and* provides hope. But the strength once derived from the certainty of faith—a certainty that perhaps was based in superstition and ignorance—has lost its power as the burdens of knowledge have weakened faith. Nevertheless, in the heart of the teacher, joy lives, and the ethical center of this book remains the teacher, whose function remains to bring human kind out of darkness.

Not superman but prophet. Not martyr, but hero. The teacher.

Notes

1. It is not uninteresting that in Tom Stoppard's play *Rosencrantz and Guildenstern are Dead* it is exactly the failure of the two to act that dooms them. One says to the other: there must have been a moment when we could have done something, said something, to assert some control over our destinies. But they have lost that moment and in the end, Rosencrantz and Guildenstern are dead.
2. Ironically, the time-span of the book is three days as well, ending not with the appearance of the human animal but with his demise and apotheosis. At his death Caldwell, like Chiron, is resurrected. The parallel to the resurrection of Jesus is obvious. This is the subject of a different essay.
3. Peter says to him, "I have hope," and Caldwell responds that he must have gotten it from his mother. But his son says, "No, from you!"

CHAPTER 6

Cabins, Pequods, and Classrooms

This cabin was no bigger than was Thoreau's dwelling on the shores of Walden Pond: both measured ten feet by fourteen feet all round. This one, wood paneled on its exterior and painted a light purplish-blue, was set back from the road behind the main house and looked out over Lake Champlain from the Vermont shore to the New York side of the water; the cabin appeared from the outside to be no more than a child's playhouse. In front of the cabin entranceway was a very small courtyard with chairs and a small table, but as it was still dead winter, I did not think I would be lounging out of doors. Fifty yards further rested the banks of Lake Champlain, and I knew no boats would be coming ashore. My retreat was assured: I could see no one and no one could see me. I had come here to enact some private business.

The inner four wood walls of the dwelling had been painted a pale, non-descript green. I supposed that the cabin was kept warm by radiant heat: the cement floor colored with a deep burgundy stain felt always warm to my bare feet when I would awaken in the middle of the night to shuffle slipperless to the bathroom. Nevertheless, during the day when I worked inside I always wore a sweater—it was February, after all, and a big snowstorm had blanketed the ground the day following my arrival. At night under the sheets and comforter I felt warm enough, but too much warmth dulls my thinking, and since when I wrote during the day I required a watchful, alert mind, I set the thermometer relatively low and worked even with one window slightly ajar to admit some cold, fresh air. At night, however, I shuttered the window.

Basically a rectangle, the cabin's interior was comprised of three distinct but contiguous areas separated essentially by two walls set so perpendicular to each other that they created the small kitchen on the southwest corner and the bathroom on the southeast corner. Between these two spaces a large closet cabinet painted picket-fence white held the few clothes and the snow boots I had brought with me. In the cabin's remaining two-thirds' space was the living quarters proper: just enough room for a queen-sized bed, a table, and two chairs. The room was capacious enough for my needs, though it seemed at times that there was not always enough space for my thoughts to unravel; at such moments I would walk to town to distract and then re-focus my mind. But usually, the room was space and opportunity enough.

As I have said, on the southwestern side of the cabin was the kitchen alcove. Here along the rear southern wall was an electric range/stove and sufficient counter space for food preparation. Actually, I did not intend the preparation of anything elaborate: I had brought along with me my metaphorical tins of canned meat—I am, in fact, a vegetarian! Atop the white formica countertop there sat a small compost pail for organic leftovers: in there I left my apple cores and coffee grounds. In the cabinets underneath the counter space were pots and pans and other kitchenware, but I prepared only boiled water. Also stored in these cabinets were an electric drip coffee machine, a percolator pot, and a French press coffee appliance. Clearly, people arrived here with their preferred brewing tools, coffee being a principal necessity. I preferred the French press device and, as I said, placed the used grounds in the tin compost pail that sat by the stovetop. In the drawers under the counter top was a generous supply of silverware and kitchen tools. A small almost inaccessible window opened out, but despite the southern exposure admitted no light.

Perpendicular to the food-preparation space and facing east was the clean-up area consisting of the steel sink, under which was a cabinet storage space with cleaning materials and containers for recyclables and a small counter space for stacking dirty dishes. I had none but a cup and a butter knife. To the left of this space was a small refrigerator, not unlike the bar fridges in hotel rooms; the one in my room was empty. Into it I placed orange juice, a stick of organic butter, and some cream for my coffee. It was sufficient. Like Thoreau, I dined out most nights. Above the sink, on two rows of shelves were dishes, water, wine, and champagne glasses (there were apparently other purposes to this cabin than that which I intended), some inexpensive ceramic coffee mugs, a toaster (I preferred my bread moist, and I did not use the appliance), and some cloth napkins.

Behind this eastern wall of the kitchen was the bathroom: a purely functional and good-sized area consisting of a toilet, a sink, and a tin shower stall. My hosts had placed containers of Dr. Bronner's liquid products as soap and shampoo supplies. Almost twenty-five years ago Dr. Bronner soaps were my choice for the household: on every bar wrapper and container of the product a manifesto was printed advocating some anarcho-Christian-Marxist-Maoist-Gandhian-Jewish-Buddhist-Islamist philosophy. Every inch of the wrapping or container was covered with writing, and since the writing was neither unitary nor continuous each portion would be positioned wherever it would fit. To read any section in full one had to keep the bottle or bar in motion. And the writing did not always make a great deal of sense: One section read: "Thank God we don't descend from perfect Adam and Eve to sinful sinner. Brother's Keeper, divided Slave! United hardworking-trained-brave, from dust we ascend up! Thank God for that! Our Brother's Teacher of the Moral ABC mason Hillel taught carpenter Jesus to unite all mankind free!" Another proclaimed, "As Mao wrote in Redbook 51: 'Marxist Communism once in power is utterly unworkable, has less value than cowdung. Its power is the gun.' As teaches African-shepherd Astronomer Israel for 6000 years, 'LISTEN CHILDREN. ETERNAL FATHER ETERNALLY ONE.' For on God's spaceship Earth, with Bomb and Gun, we're all one or none. All-one. All-one. Exceptions eternally. Absolute none." I understood almost nothing of what Dr. Bronner spoke, but I did not doubt his passion or sincerity. With a labeled product of Dr. Bronner's soap, going to the bathroom was transformed into a complete spiritual experience, and there was little need to carry in, as was my wont, a magazine, book, or Sudoku.

I have started describing the cabin from its southern end because most of what seemed to be the formal business end of it existed there. However, just to the north of the kitchen/bathroom section was the living space proper. A queen-sized bed sat in the middle of the room with its headboard bumped up along the western wall. In fact, the bed took up most of the room's space. On either side of the headboard was a night table: on the right was a stool-like stand that held books that had been left, I suppose, by previous occupants, and next to that table stood a wooden-spindle reading lamp. On the other side of the bedside was a more spacious and proper night table: it was round with a glass top on which sat a gooseneck reading lamp. On this table I could place my reading glasses, my night medicines, a glass of water, and the current book. Four pillows rested against the headboard and upon which at night I rested my head.

At the foot of the bed was a small wooden ladder table. Here during the day I would set up the laptop computer and write. I sat in a less than comfortable rocking chair, but I understood that this cabin had not been structured to be a work environment. There was in the space a white wicker chair as well—this cabin was clearly meant for two—but this chair was too deep to be able to occupy it and still reach the tabletop. *C'est tout* for the basic floor furniture.

The walls were not bare: on the southern wall of the cabin and beside the bed was a framed fourteen by eighteen inch acrylic romanticized painting of a run-down and abandoned stone cottage nestled somewhere in a copse of thick green trees. The scene seemed to reflect a late afternoon because the front face of the cottage shone with a deep rust color, almost as if it had been burned from exposure to the sun. The entranceway to the cabin gaped wide and irregular; this wreck was not the work of human renovation but of nature's deconstruction. No door remained to obstruct entrance, and the stonework had all fallen away. The doorway to the cottage had long ago broken and decayed: it now looked more like an entrance to a barn than to a home. Or the absent doorway seemed in appearance like a gaping toothless mouth. Above the absent door was a single paneless window. Clearly, no one any longer occupied this cabin. Van Gogh in Arles might have painted the scene if he had been a very bad painter. Perhaps the painting had been purchased for its thematic import, but it seemed to me notably unnoteworthy and uncharacteristic of this Northern setting. The colors, the trees, and the sunlight seem more appropriate to the Caribbean than to Northern Vermont.

On the cabin's northern wall was a small poster-like print, no larger than ten inches by twelve inches, by an artist named dug nap. dug nap is a local celebrity and his prints are ubiquitous in Burlington. The prints are all executed in exactly the same style but the saying on each is different and they are meant to be socially relevant and clever. Normally a very upward-looking person, my daughter owns two of them, one that reads "Down with Underpants" and the other "Down with Toilet Seats." The one in my cottage said "Less is the New More." That seemed appropriate here somehow despite my slight pique with what I deemed too much clutter.

I did not lack for sunlight. On the northern wall were two rectangular windows almost a yard high and over a foot wide; each contained six sparkling glass panels. Between the windows and centered on the northern wall was a glass paneled door which allowed light to enter and gave me egress to an expansive yard that overlooked Lake Champlain across which were the mountains of New York State. This particular morning across the waters the sun lit up the mountaintops like candle flames.

I have always felt that the attempts to describe a space in words seemed an impossible task. My description above confirms my thought: I know exactly what the space looked like, and the reader might have gathered some sense of geography, proportion, and color, but perhaps I mean more to have been able to offer a sense of how the space *felt*. It was a home to me for the week that I spent there.

What was I doing here? Why did I choose the shack as my *destination*, the latter a word that maintains some intimate connection to *destiny*? What private business did I mean to effect?

I think that I thought that as I had recently scheduled my social security payments to begin, it was time to leave home. Thoreau (1960) says, "It is remarkable how easily and insensibly we fall into a particular route, and make a beaten track for ourselves . . . The surface of the earth is soft and impressible by the feet of men; and so with the paths which the mind travels . . . I did not wish to take a cabin passage, but rather to go before the mast and on the deck of the world, for there I could best see the moonlight amid the mountains. I do not wish to go below now." For years I have allowed the anticipation of sea-sickness to keep me landlocked, and it was time, I thought, to head out to sea. For not a few years I have suffered, I believe, from a mild form of agoraphobia: fear of wide spaces. I somewhere read that the agoraphobe's fear might derive in part from the experience in these seemingly ever-widening spaces of being incapable of maintaining a sense of control. Out *there* exist too many possibilities, too much contingency, too many uncertainties necessitating quick decision. I suspect that agoraphobia might serve as an accompanying condition to Obsessive

Compulsive Disorder: I have somehow in my life learned to appreciate my ducks recognizable and in order. Out *there* in those wide-open spaces too many roads diverged into too many yellow woods; out *there* I experienced too much anxiety, even fear: out *there* I felt threatened by too many necessary selections and too much ambiguity.

So to this agoraphobe it seemed best not to venture out into such imagined chaos. At home, surrounded by my books, my familiar furniture, and ready access to nourishment, I could preserve an imaginary sense of control over my immediate needs and anticipated wants, and for some years this comfort had allowed me to avoid venturing very far from home. At some time in my late thirties I ceased to want to travel much distance: three hours in a car seemed to be the extent of my ability to wander. Nevertheless, I was at present suffering from an overwhelming sense of feeling entrapped by my incapacity to leave home. And the winds had blown hard against me; I had crashed on the rocks of the Lee Shore. And so, as one of the first adventures on a recent sabbatical leave, I boarded ship and headed out to a place with which I had some familiarity, where I had acquaintance with a person or two, but where also I would be alone, on my own, and away from all of the conveniences I possessed at home. I shipped on board my whaling vessel and headed out to sea on land. I wanted to see if I could write or think while away from my books, my comforts, my electric gas fireplace. I had some private business to conduct. I rented the cabin for a week.

II

I think that we all seek some peace and refuge from the world's turmoil. In J. B. Coates' gospel song, the soul finds its shelter in faith in the Lord who will provide some comfort here at death's approach. But I think that here on this earth in this present moment there are more regular and less final seekings. On a daily basis, many like me imagine the existence of some haven to where we might go in retreat from what we consider the slings and arrows of outrageous fortune. Perhaps how and where we seek that refuge somehow allows us to define ourselves: some block out the world's noise by turning up the local volume, some take to drink and drugs, some make a remove to the seclusion of the cloistered life, and others retreat into the stacks of libraries. Some go to the cabin!

For some time I have been thinking about how the spaces of cabins and shacks illusorily offer some promise of such refuge for our souls. In the mid-west where I live, on any Wednesday afternoon, when queried about weekend plans my neighbors say with some pride and relief, "We're going to the cabin!" Sometimes those cabins are situated relatively near—a drive of an hour or two—but some cabins are located in far distant places—sometimes many hours from the daily dwelling. Total travel time on a weekend to the cabin and back itself could sometimes equate to a whole day's retreat. For longer flights, pilgrims pack the car with the necessities to sustain them for several weeks—the approximate length of most vacation stays. Some of these "cabins" are equal in size to their everyday houses, and these cabins (indeed, most cabins with which I am familiar) possess all of the modern conveniences that belong to those other daily residences: telephones and flat-screen televisions, large food freezers, wide front lawns that require maintenance, laptop computers (at least), and wireless internet access. And on the ponds and lakes on the shores of which the cabins sit, the din of the motorboats disrupts the quiet, and water skiers flash into and out of the fields of vision. These cabins are meant as a getaway: yet when I imagine the necessary maintenance and expense these places require, and the clutter and noise of the environment in which these cabins suffer, I am reminded of Bob Dylan's plaint in "Not Dark Yet": "I can't even remember what it was I came here to get away from." In the woods behind the cabins, hikers each march to the beat of their own iPods. Nevertheless, the myth of the cabin figures centrally in the American consciousness as a place for escape. I have become skeptical of these refuges as places to go.

In these spaces we call cabins, away from the daily occupations, the familiar streets and stores and neighbors, the weary travelers mean to slip off the cares of the messy quotidian and live there unencumbered by the stuff of this world. "Simplicity, simplicity, simplicity!" Thoreau urged. "I say, let your affairs be as two or three, and not a hundred or a thousand; instead of a million count half a dozen, and keep your accounts on your thumbnail" (1960, 66), but too often at these cabins the to-do lists clutter the spaces. Nevertheless, the lore and lure of the mythical cabin is simplicity recovered, though as I have suggested there is often nothing simple about the presence of too many of these refuges. From these fabled retreats, the daily burdens that encase the selves and deny them growth are meant to be sloughed off and discarded. In these cabins weary travelers mean to enjoy the opportunity to cleanse and renew themselves for yet another troubled essay into our encumbered daily lives. For those living in cramped city environments or manicured suburbs, and to those working confined in crowded office complexes and noisy, dirty factories, these cabins illusorily promise some respite from the stifling noise and clutter of the diurnal: in these places, it is believed, there will be space and sometimes quiet enough to read and to write, time and energy to engage in solitary thought, "to learn to reawaken and keep ourselves awake, not by mechanical aids, but by an infinite expectation of the dawn . . ." (65). Sometimes at the cabin the weary pilgrims plumb the depths for fish: Thoreau somewhere said that many men go fishing all of their lives without knowing that it is not fish they are after. These cabins are places, it is held, where the peace may come dropping slow. Though really, too often when I inquire of the experience of these cabin owners it seems to me that they speak too much of clutter and noise.

Though this essay is not meant as a sociological or cultural history of the cabin, I believe that the myth of the cabin as refuge runs throughout Anglo-American and even Judeo-Christian culture, the cabin serving as some escape from the oppressive daily world burdened by duty, industrialization, and capital. God commands Jonah to journey to Nineveh on a mission to warn the city of its imminent destruction, "but Jonah started to run away from the Lord's presence." Seeking to avoid the world and his mission in it, Jonah took refuge aboard a ship, paid his fare, and "went below deck and fell asleep" even as a heavy storm at sea threatened to break up the ship and drown all the sailors. "The men rowed hard to regain the shore, but they could not, for the sea was growing more and more stormy about them." Jonah had effectively retreated into a cabin-like space from the world that oppressed him. But he was not saved. When the sailors learned that Jonah was fleeing from responsibility, they inquired what they could do to allay the storm. And Jonah, knowing that the storm resulted from his attempt to seek refuge from the world, advised the sailors to abandon him. And the sailors "heaved Jonah overboard, and the sea stopped raging."

William Wordsworth, in his sonnet "The World is too Much With Us," bemoans a world where "late and soon/getting and spending" have laid waste our natural powers: he protests that we have become alienated from our world and have abandoned our sympathy with Nature. That natural world for which Wordsworth longs is not one in which we merely subsist, but rather, is a world in which we continually come into being. Wordsworth's complaint is what sends Sigurd Olson (1997) and Thoreau to their cabins and what leads Wordsworth to an adoration of Nature. And at the center of this world sits the cabin as the omphalos of Nature. In his autobiographical poem *The Prelude*, Wordsworth writes not of the cabin *per se*, but of the peace that the cabin in the heart of Nature offers to the city-oppressed:

> With deep devotion, Nature, did I feel,
> In that enormous City's turbulent world
> Of men and things, what benefit I owed
> To thee, and those domains of rural peace
> Where to the sense of beauty first my heart
> Was opened
>   (70–75).

It is the noise of the city that has stopped the poet's ears to the peace and beauty of Nature, and it is the peace available in the nature-cabin that the poet seeks as refuge for his soul, as his place to listen and to serve. Wordsworth complains that we have become strangers in a strange land.

> Great God! I'd rather be
> A Pagan suckled in a creed outworn;
> So might I, standing on this pleasant lea,
> Have glimpses that would make me less forlorn;
> Have sight of Proteus rising from the sea;
> Or hear old Triton blow his wreathed horn
>   (ll. 9–14).

But, alas, the poet has not yet achieved that place: his plaint is evidence enough of his discontent. Apparently, Wordsworth's two-story home at Grasmere in the Lake District seemed not to be the cabin to which he might make his retreat; the world remained even here still too much with him, and he, like we, had become too sophisticated, as it were, too worldly, and had seemingly lost touch with the creative primitive and wild that residency of the cabin offered.

 This imagined loss of Nature as a source of original inspiration might be located in part in the Enlightenment emphasis on

Reason as the means by which everything might be known and by which all questions might be answered. But a heavy price had to be paid for this advance. For Giambattista Vico, the eighteenth-century Italian political philosopher and historian (in Berlin, 2013, 161), "the increase in humanity and knowledge . . . is inevitably accompanied by a loss of primitive vigour, directness, imaginative force, beyond any made possible by the development of the critical intellect." Berlin (147) notes that Vico and the romantics such as Wordsworth held that in our modern times rational reflection had taken the place of instinct, imagination, and types of knowing "not analysable except in terms of itself, nor can it be identified save by examples." The ideal cabin came to serve as the escape from the reality of the library and laboratory where original, unmediated experience might be enjoyed. In his autobiographical poem *The Prelude*, Wordsworth despairs that

> . . . demanding formal *proof*
> And seeking it in everything, I lost
> All feeling of conviction, and, in fine,
> Sick, wearied out with contrarities,
> Yielded up moral questions in despair
> (Book 11, 301–305).

For Wordsworth, reason proved to be of least use where it was most needed: determining what was good and what was evil rather than distinguishing mere right from wrong. The myth of the cabin in the midst of Nature offered respite from this oppression.

Berlin claims that the type of knowledge for which Vico (and Wordsworth) advocated is that which is "involved when a work of the imagination or of social diagnosis or a work of criticism or scholarship or history is described not as correct or incorrect, skilful or inept, a success or a failure, but as profound or shallow, realistic or unrealistic, perceptive or stupid, alive or dead" (2013, 148). That is, the knowledge to which Vico refers is a knowledge realized by direct acquaintance with an "inner state," or by a sympathetic insight into the states of others and derives from *imaginative* as opposed to *rational* power. The cabin offered such experience. Worsdworth says that

> From Nature doth emotion come, and moods
> Of calmness equally are Nature's gift:
> This is her glory; these two attributes
> Are sister horns that constitute her strength.
> Hence Genius, born to thrive by interchange
> Of peace and excitation, finds in her
> His best and purest friend; from her receives
> That energy by which he seeks the truth,
> From her that happy stillness of the mind
> Which fits him to receive it when unsought
>   (Book 13, 1–10).

Thoreau (1961, 61) had protested that "Gardening is civil and social, but it wants the vigor and freedom of the forest and the outlaw." There ought to be little place for gardens at the cabin, and though for one year Thoreau maintained a bean field, after the first harvest he vowed not to plant beans the next year. He had, he suggested, other seeds to sow, "as sincerity, truth, simplicity, faith, innocence, and the like, and see if they will not grow in this soil, even with less toil and manurance, and sustain me, for surely it has not been exhausted for these crops" (113). As Wordsworth had contended, Thoreau insisted that we have in our reliance on Reason become too civilized and have lost an original relationship to the earth. Thoreau (210) writes, "The very uprightness of the pines and maples asserts the ancient rectitude and vigor of nature. Our lives need the relief of such a background, where the pine flourishes and the jay screams." So does Wordsworth in his sonnet long for the opportunity in nature and at the cabin to relieve the alienation he experiences; Wordsworth desires in Thoravian terms, to "see, smell, taste, hear, feel, that everlasting Something to which we are allied, at once our maker, our abode, our destiny, our very Selves . . ." (213). The cabin as retreat is the romantic destination to which the wearied traveler might effect that escape and make return.

That cabin that rests mythically only in the imagination arose, I speculate, during the eighteenth century in that conflict between the rationalist enterprise and the spiritual opposition to it. Berlin (2000, 260) quotes the German metaphysician Friedrich Heinrich Jacobi: "The light is in my heart; as soon as I try to carry it to my intellect, it goes out." The cabin was the place where that little light of mine might continue to shine. Jean-Jacques Rousseau pleaded against the artificiality of the rules of rationalism and scientific method as a means of knowing the world. Berlin (2000, 252) writes: "Rousseau's impassioned pleas for direct vision and natural feeling, his denunciation of the artificial social roles which civilisation forces men to play against the true ends and needs of their natures, his idealisation of more primitive, spontaneous human societies, his contrast between natural self-expression and the crippling artificiality of social divisions and conventions which rob men of dignity and freedom, and promote privilege, power and arbitrary bullying at one end of the human scale, and humiliating obsequiousness at the other . . ." epitomizes the appeal of the cabin. It is by the deeply held myth that at the cabin relief from the diurnal world may be experienced, though I suspect that this relief be only imaginary.

The Romantics held that the cabin, free from social influence and constraint, was the place where the strait jackets society tightened on the individual might be undone and the unfettered self might then expand and develop under its own power. This myth pervades the escape to the cabin still prevalent today. In the cabin the self achieves an authenticity that reason had ironically falsified and over which the industrial world had paved. But when the world that is too much with us late and soon came to occupy the space of the cabin, then the myth of the cabin retreat became unsustainable: the haven the cabin offered became unreachable and its peace inaccessible. The cabin became a name and ceased being a place. Wordsworth, loathe to abandon his faith in Nature and the natural, sought to somehow reconcile the romantic image of the cabin as redemptive retreat with the power of Reason offered by the Enlightenment thinkers. As Wordsworth ironically discovers, the peace sought in the cabin could be available to the adult *only* in thought! The actual cabin sanctuary was no longer possible or even necessary.

In Wordsworth's "Intimations Ode," the poet reconciles the myth of the cabin—in the poem associated with the innocence and joy of childhood—with the rationalist enterprise of the Enlightenment, and he affirms that the idea of the cabin serves for the adult not as *refuge* from the world but as the place where *in thought* the original relation to the world of nature may be recovered! The cabin becomes truly imagined and results from a state of mind: it might even be experienced in the midst of the world too much with us! The poet writes that this loss of the natural relation and the ideal embodied in the myth of the cabin is inevitable, and that "though nothing will bring back that hour of splendour in the grass," yet, "in thought" we can recover the joy and wisdom that only the child knows but lacks the words to articulate. The cabin is no panacea for that loss, but through words written, we adults can *in thought* experience the joy and original relationship with the universe that the child enjoys in fact. One creates the peace of the cabin wherever one engages *in thought*. The poet wonders, "Where is that visionary gleam to be found?"

> We *in thought* will join your throng
> ....
> We will grieve not, rather find
> Strength in what remains behind;
> In the primal sympathy
> Which having been must ever be;

> In the soothing thoughts that spring out of human suffering;
> In the faith that looks through death,
> In years that bring the philosophic mind (italics added)
> (ll. 171, 179–186).

The alienation and oppressiveness of this world too much with us late and soon can be held at bay *in thought: in thought* one can experience the intimations of immortality available actually to the child. Such alone is the comfort of the adult. It is not the cabin in which peace might be restored because as adults we may be out of reach of such resource, but for now the peace we seek might come dropping slow in the subjective realm of thought.

> Hence in a season of calm weather
> Though inland far we be,
> Our souls have sight of that immortal sea
> Which brought us hither,
> Can in a moment travel thither,
> And see the Children sport upon the shore,
> And hear the mighty waters rolling evermore
> (ll.161–167).

Wherever we might find ourselves, we may in thought recognize what once we were and possessed as children, and in that perception *think* our way back to that time of unity and that moment of splendour in the grass to which we may never again return in fact but only in thought.

As much as they are physical places, cabins and shacks seem to be psychological spaces, locations that occur as much *in the mind* as in the actual world. There exists a conventional understanding that cabins and shacks serve as a form of retreat from the daily spaces in which we regularly suffer from the stresses and difficulties that attend our lives out in the world. Such may be said about the origin of Yeats' cabin of clay and wattles built on the Lake Isle of Inisfree. Of it Yeats writes,

> I will arise and go now, for always night and day
> I hear lake water lapping with low sounds by the shore;
> While I stand on the roadway, or on the pavements grey,
> I hear it in the deep heart's core.

Yeats' cabin of clay and wattles subsists *only* in his imagination: in the present the poet stands trapped on the macadamized roadway in the midst of civilization. It is only in his mind that the cabin endures as the place where the peace might come dropping slow.

Bob Dylan, too, speaks of such an imagined place in his composition, "Sign on the Window." After detailing the tensions and displeasures of his life in the city, he longs to:

> Build me a cabin in Utah
> Marry me a wife, catch rainbow trout
> Have a bunch of kids who call me "Pa"
> That must be what it's all about
> That must be what it's all about.

It is the myth of simplicity to which Dylan alludes, one to which he might have been introduced in part from school history classes or from sitting in front of the television sets and radios of his youth. Not unlike the myth of the little red schoolhouse—that was neither red nor pleasant but that continues to linger as our romantic image of a past that did not exist—Dylan's cabin in Utah, like Yeats' cabin on Inisfree, serves as an imaginary retreat to a place to which that world does not enter, where the cares of daily life may be sloughed off as a snake rids itself of its too-tight skin, and where children run safe, happy, and free. Of course, the possibility of that retreat is as false as is the idea of the West to which at the novel's end Huck Finn flees ahead of the rest to avoid a civilization epitomized in Aunt Polly's disciplines. Huck's is a doomed retreat: as Thoreau well knew, the Fitchburg Railroad did roar by the shores of Walden Pond. But despite the constant incursion of the complex on the simple, the cabin remains in our mythology as a symbol of an imagined physical and psychic escape. I have grown skeptical of the efficacy of these cabins and the peace they offer.

SOME OTHER CABINS I HAVE KNOWN

Conventionally, nevertheless, the myth of the cabin persists: inside these shacks one is meant to experience a profound and productive solitude, peace, and quiet. And the cabin need not be in fact an actual cabin though it is a physical space. In Jane Austen's *Mansfield Park* there exists within the great mansion on the estate of Mansfield Park in the physicality of a single room the psychological facsimile of the shack. It is into that room that Fanny Price retreats. "She could go there after anything unpleasant below, and find immediate consolation in some pursuit, or some train of thought at hand. Her plants, her books . . . her writing desk, and her works of charity and ingenuity, were all within her reach; or if indisposed for employment, if nothing but musing would do, she could scarcely see an object in that room which had not an interesting remembrance connected with it. Everything was a friend, or bore her thoughts to a friend" (Austen, 2004, 133). In that room all becomes right again: in that room "The whole was now so blended together, so harmonized by distance, that every former affliction had its charm." Here in Fanny's room is Wordsworth's Nature, Yeats' peace, and Dylan's cabin. In this "shack" Fanny would retire to be alone, to recover her stability, and to ready herself to return to the complex world with which she daily dealt.

For Virginia Woolf that cabin was a room of one's own. "Get yourself," she urges her audience that here consisted almost wholly of women, "a room of your own and five hundred a year" (2005, 109). In a language not unlike that of Thoreau, Woolf urges the women that from that room of one's own she could "live in the presence of reality, an invigorating life, it would appear, whether one can impart it or not" (109). It is in that room of one's own—the cabin—that one gathers the energy to live in the world even if in that room of one's own she cannot write about either the world or the experience of the room. Woolf urges that in that room of one's own one might "dream over books and loiter at street corners and let the line of thought dip deep into the stream." Interestingly, Thoreau had earlier said that *time* was the stream in which he fished, but for Woolf it is into the cabin that she would throw her line. In Woolf's room the Enlightenment ideal persists that in that room of one's own one could *think* oneself to freedom and creativity even if one could not return in fact to that moment of the splendour in the grass. In those rooms the world would be explored, considered, and invented. Woolf writes, "For my belief is that if we live another century or so—I am talking of the common life which is the real life and not of the little separate lives which we live as individuals—and have five hundred a year each of us *and rooms of our own*; if we have the habit of freedom and the courage to write exactly what we think; if we escape a little from the common sitting-room and see human beings not always in their relation to each other but in relation to reality . . . if we face the fact, for it is a fact, that there is no arm to cling to, but that we go alone and that our relation is to the world of reality and not only to the world of men and women, then the opportunity will come and the dead poet who was Shakespeare's sister will put on the body which she has so often laid down" (112, italics added). It is in the cabin where such work might be done.

These cabins promised relief from the world too much with us late and soon; these cabins offered renewal and rebirth. For Olson,

Listening Point, a small, glaciated piece of rock, like the shores of Walden Pond, is the place where he could transact some private business. Olson writes (1997, 8), "I named this place Listening Point because only when one comes to listen, only when one is aware and still, can things be seen and heard. Everyone has a listening-point somewhere. It does not have to be in the north, but some place of quiet where the universe can be contemplated with awe." It was here on Listening Point that the world too much with him could be cast off and where "this remnant of the old wilderness would speak to me of silence and solitude, of belonging and wonder and beauty." Listening Point seems to be the place to which Olson might retreat to reestablish an original relationship to the universe, where he might "renew the sense of mystery and wonder and even some of the dreams" that our ancestors once had known before the clutter of the world intervened. Thus it was on Listening Point that Olson constructed his cabin as the fixed point from which that journeying would lead. Indeed, that cabin was a place not to which he retired but from which he ventured! "From the very beginning of our adventure with the point, we had dreamed of someday having a little cabin tucked back in the pines, a place we could come to on a moment's notice without having to bother with food and equipment; a simple shelter where we could just move in, spend a few hours, a night or two, or if in the mood even a week, an outpost away from the phone and interruptions" (17). Like Thoreau's cabin at Walden Pond, the cabin at Listening Point was a return to originality and simplicity, but from which he might journey out to exploration.

In Roth's *I Married a Communist,* several shacks exist and serve as places of refuge from the world. Ira Ringold, the communist referred to in the title, lives daily in bustling and complicated New York City but maintains a two-room shack up in Zinc Town, New Jersey. It is to that shack that Ira flees when he needs to recover a self he feels he has lost. Zuckerman writes, "Ira retreated to Zinc Town to live not so much close to nature as close to the bone, to live life in the raw, swimming in the mud pond right into November, tramping the woods on snowshoes in coldest winter, or, on rainy days, meandering around in his Jersey car—a used '39 coupe—talking to the local dairy farmers and the old zinc miners, whom he tried to get to understand how they were being screwed by the system." The shack was a place to which Ira could return to to reinforce the image of himself as just another working stiff, though, in fact, he had married the famous actress Eve Frame and lived a luxurious and even prominent and public life as the radio star Iron Rinn in a town house in the West Village. Ira's shack was where he would go in retreat from the world that had become too much with him late and soon. Zuckerman writes, "The shack furnished an antidote to West Eleventh Street and an asylum from West Eleventh Street, the place where you go to sweat out the bad vapors" (Roth, 1998, 51). But the world followed Ira out to the shack: Eve hated the shack in all its rawness and simplicity and begged Ira that she be allowed to renovate the shack replete with a room for her daughter and Ira's nemesis, Sylphide. When the world threatened to invade the retreat, Ira exploded: "Then screw it . . . The house won't be lovely. The house will be shitty. Fuck the whole project [of renovation]" (248). Finally, following the scandal over Eve's book, Ira makes a last retreat to the shack, and it is there that, ironically I think, his aorta bursts.

If for Ira the shack was a place of retreat, then for Zuckerman the shack becomes a sheltered cloister. The cabin is where Zuckerman had come to live in seclusion after having achieved both fame and notoriety after publishing his novel *Carnovsky*. For Zuckerman the cabin becomes his walled retreat from the world that had, indeed, become too much with him late and soon. Zuckerman writes, "I wondered if Murray had as yet recognized my house as an upgraded replica of the two-room shack on the Jersey side of the Delaware Water Gap that was Ira's beloved retreat . . . Though I had been looking for something larger and more conventionally a house, I bought it right off. 'Hermit here—back off,' the owner's state of mind was discernible in the absence of anything like a patch across the hay field that led to the bolted front door" (71). Within the walls of his cabin, Zuckerman in chosen solitude writes and reads, and except for brief forays into town for food and other essentials, and save for his human contact in the single semester class he teaches at Athena College, Zuckerman does not leave his cabin. Except for Murray's porch visits over six summer evenings, Zuckerman does not invite many in and does not venture too far out. There is no world in Zuckerman's cabin: there is only Zuckerman and the work of his imagination. There is no world outside into which he would venture.

III

But from my experience with cabins and from some of my reading, I have begun to speculate: what if the peace imagined to be available in the cabin or in Nature was not at all a source of spiritual revival? What if the cabin and raw nature were not meant at all as havens from the world that was with us too much late and soon? What if even in rational thought the peace and security of childhood remained unavailable? What if the allure of the cabin was nothing more than the treacherous voice of the Siren? What if the imagined retreat into the cabin was nothing more than a dangerous delusion? In the chapter "The Mast-Head," (Melville, 1962, 153) Ishmael offers some hint of the dangerous and deceptively innocent allures that the myth of escape of the cabin offered. "There you stand," Ishmael writes, of the sailor at his post in the mast-head, "lost in the infinite series of the sea, with nothing ruffled but the waves. The tranced ship indolent rolls; the drowsy trade winds blow; everything resolves you into languor . . . a sublime uneventfulness invests you; you hear no news, read no gazettes; extras with startling accounts of commonplaces never delude you into unncessary excitements; you hear of no domestic afflictions, bankrupt securities; fall of stocks, are never troubled with the thought of what you shall have for dinner. . . ." Here Melville presents the mast-head of the ship as a continuation of the myth of the cabin as a refuge from the world too much with us late and soon, and as in the myth of the cabin, this mast-head promises welcome relief from the slings and arrows of outrageous fortune. Up in the mast-head, many may go seeking that refuge for the soul.

But, Ishmael warns, the imagined escape is illusory and fraught with danger. The complaint that his shipmates make of the distrait sailor is that during his time in the mast-head he is not present to the world and the "whales are as scarce as hen's teeth whenever thou art up there" (156). The Pequod is, after all, hunting whales for a livelihood, and the success of the voyage depends on the attentiveness of the man atop the mast-head! Ishmael asserts that though the whale fisheries offer to the "romantic, melancholy and absent-minded young men, disgusted with the carking cares of the earth" the fantasy of escape, these young men who stand aloft in the mast-head are soon "lulled into an opium-like listlessness of vacant, unconscious reverie . . . by the blending cadence of waves with thought, that at last he loses his identity . . ." The mast-head becomes a dangerous opiate, and there is great menace in the illusory escape it offers. Aloft in the mast-head "while this sleep, this dream is on ye, move your foot or hand an inch; slip your hand at all; and your identity comes back in horror. Over Descartian vortices you hover. And perhaps, at mid-day, in the fairest weather, with one half-throttled shriek you drop through that transparent air into the summer sea, no more to rise for ever" (157). Though it promises peaceful escape, this cabin-like space, in fact, threatens ones very existence unless rapt attention is paid aloft there. Up in the mast-head, the loss of the world puts at risk the loss of life. The cabin here is not so much a refuge as a perilous allure.

Know ye Bulkington? Ishmael first sees Bulkington at the Spouter Inn in New Bedford, the city to which Ishmael has journeyed to sign on board a whaling ship for a hunting voyage that will extend for several years. Ishmael discloses that it is to the sea that he heads whenever he finds himself "growing grim about the mouth; whenever it is a damp, drizzly November in my soul; whenever I find myself involuntarily pausing before coffin warehouses, and bringing up the rear of every funeral I meet; and especially whenever my hypos get such an upper hand of me, that it requires a strong moral principle to prevent me from deliberately stepping into the street, and methodically knocking people's hats off . . ." (12). Ishmael's enlistment onboard the Pequod is not his first sea voyage, nor do I think that that tragic venture had been his final such journey. There is something about the land, maybe it is the teeming town—but *not* the world too much with us late and soon—that oppresses Ishmael, and from which he demands relief. It has been said that Ishmael suffers from depression—zoloft, welbutrin, or paxil might have served him well, it might be argued—but I think it is motives quite different than depression or retreat that send Ishmael out to sea.

In "Loomings," our introduction to Ishmael, we get further hint of his motives. There Ishmael suggests that it is to the sea that *all* men and women head almost instinctively: as he walks about in the cities he finds "thousands upon thousands of mortal men fixed in ocean reveries," searching for the soul's refuge. Ishmael suggests that it is to the water that all paths to some illusory peace seem to lead, but Ishmael's paean to that imagined harmony concludes with the story of Narcissus who, looking into the water "could not grasp the tormenting, mild image he saw in the fountain, plunged into it and was drowned." That is, Narcissus imagined that he saw in the water the peace that comes dropping slow, and reaching for it, he lost his life. Seeking escape from the world that was too much with them late and soon, these souls look to the sea, but indeed, such refuge may not be found there. Ishmael reflects that what Narcissus saw in the waters in the fountain "we ourselves see in all rivers and oceans. It is the image of the ungraspable phantom of life; and this is the key to all." But that the image is ungraspable remains central: though they might seek they will never find, and these mortal men and women will continue their lives in restlessness and unhappiness while seeking that which could not be held. In their reveries they imagine an end to their lives of quiet desperation, and thus refrain from an engagement in the vital struggle that existence demands *if* true freedom is to be achieved. This, I think, is what Ishmael learns aboard his cabin—the Pequod. Ishmael is a learner, and perhaps the Pequod his cabin.

But unlike the peace of Yeats' cabin of clay and wattles made where the peace comes dropping slow, Ishmael's life aboard the ship at sea demands constant vigilance and effort: he chooses to go to sea as a common sailor and not as captain. Having once been a schoolmaster, Ishmael has abandoned that role of leader he had held on land—the one who knows—for the position of the sailor—the one who seeks—upon the seeming illimitable and elusive expanses of the sea. Knowing he heads to sea in search of something, he enlists as a common sailor, Ishmael admits, because "[i]t is quite as much as I can do to take care of myself, without taking care of ships, barques, brigs, schooners, and what not" (3). Further, Ishmael's choice to go to sea as only a sailor is motivated not only by the need for pay but also because he benefits from "the wholesome exercise and pure air of the forecastle deck." As a sailor, Ishmael says, the air he breathes is fresh and original, unlike that of the captain who from his position behind the forecastle deck must breathe the air second hand. Aboard ship—in this instance, aboard the Pequod—Ishmael confronts life immediately, as do from their cabins in their slightly different ways Wordsworth, Thoreau, and Olson. The Pequod appears in this instance, to my mind, the image of the cabin! But this cabin exists not as a place of retreat or refuge but as a medium for exploration, requiring effort and even threatening danger.

Ishmael's motives for this time choosing a whaling voyage on which to enlist—he goes to sea usually, he admits, as a merchant sailor—seem at first unknowable to him. "Though I cannot tell why it was exactly those stage managers, the Fates, put me down for this shabby part of a whaling voyage," Ishmael speculates that it was the image of the whale, that awesome beast which had been the object of wonder throughout history, that sends him to New Bedford. And it is also true that the journey of the whaling vessel, its sense of danger, exoticness, and strangeness, attracts this quester. So it is with Ishmael. "I am tormented with an everlasting itch for things remote. I love to sail forbidden seas, and land on barbarous coasts. Not ignoring what is good, I am quick to perceive a horror, and could still be social with it—would they let me—since it is but well to be on friendly terms with all the inmates of the place one lodges in" (6). Once a schoolmaster and always a student, Ishmael enlists on board the Pequod because it is there that the world in its full register of values may be best experienced and explored in the pursuit of that awesome, magnificent, and enigmatic creature, the whale. Not at all a place for retreat, the Pequod becomes the cabin from which to engage with the world's mysteries, and from where Ishmael might learn from that struggle. This passion for knowledge explains the appearance in the opening pages of the manuscript, "Etymologies," which offers glimpses of the speculations of others throughout history concerning the whales that the Pequod hunts: these creatures have been and are yet a great mystery that attracts those such as Ishmael. Ishmael is a learner.

KNOW YE BULKINGTON?

Know ye Bulkington? Ishmael was at once drawn to Bulkington. At the Spouter Inn that first evening in New Bedford, a boisterous and festive spirit prevailed amongst the sailors home from the sea, but Ishmael characteristically does not partake in the revelry. As he stands about the edges of the crowd at the inn, Ishmael's gaze is drawn toward another—to Bulkington, who also stands on the fringes of the festivities. Ishmael (14) describes him: "I have seldom seen such brawn in a man. His face was deeply brown and burnt, making his white teeth dazzling by the contrast; while in the deep shadows of his eyes floated some reminscences that did not seem to give him much joy." I think that what attracts Ishmael to this man who remained on the peripheries of the party is the visage that suggests that Bulkington does not spend a great deal of time indoors or that he has neither partaken of much casual pleasure nor experienced life thoughtlessly. Bulkington, I think, has not retreated to the real or metaphorical cabin. Like Ishmael, Bulkington must have spent a great deal of time out of doors; given his visage and location, he must ship often aboard ship. His look suggests some essential knowledge, though whatever it is that flows through Bulkington's mind does not seem to provide him with much pleasure. Ishmael intuits a depth to Bulkington which intrigues and attracts Ishmael, and of course offers insight into the character of the man the reader is directed to call Ishmael, the son who was cast out and sent to live in the desert. But this is the only mention of Bulkington in the chapter, because at some point on that first night, when the party at the inn became too animated, Ishmael comments that Bulkington has slipped away.

Know ye Bulkington? It is not until Chapter 23, after the Pequod has set off on its long whaling sea-voyage and made Ishmael and Bulkington shipmates, that Bulkington reappears in the narrative. Noting his presence on deck, Ishmael looks with sympathetic awe and fearfulness upon this man who in the midst of winter had returned from a dangerous four-year voyage, only to immediately sign aboard the Pequod to undertake an extended journey in the dangerous enterprise of hunting whales. Such is Bulkington that ye *should* know him. Though nothing about Ishmael suggests any engagement in any serious, much less intimate, conversation with Bulkington, Ishmael seems to intuit a sympathy between the two shipmates. Ishmael acknowledges that both men understand the allure that the bosom of the land offers, and both concede what concord, community, and companionship might be available there. Nonetheless, both men also acknowledge the danger to life and soul that such illusory harbor represents. Of Bulkington Ishamel writes:

> Let me only say that it fared with him as with the storm-tossed ship, that miserably drives along the leeward land. The port would fain give succor; the port is pitiful; in the port is safety, comfort, hearthstone, supper, warm blankets, friends, all that's kind to our mortalities. But in that gale, the port, the land, is that ship's direst jeopardy; she must fly all hospitality; one touch of land, though it but graze the keel, would make her shudder through and through. With all her might she crowds all sail off shore; in so doing, fights 'gainst the very winds that fain would blow her homeward; seeks all the lashed sea's landlessness again; for refuge's sake forlornly rushing into peril; her only friend her bitterest foe!

I think that for Ishmael what defines Bulkington is his engagement with the struggle that the life of the sea represents; it is this effort that keeps Bulkington—and eventually Ishmael—on the fringes of society. In just the same way that Thoreau's cabin maintains his status as an outsider and a purveyor of huckleberries, so does the Pequod—or whatever boat on which they ship—keep Bulkington and Ishmael on society's fringes. I think that it is this restlessness that provokes Ishmael's enlistment to persistently head out to sea and that attracted him at once to Bulkington. Both, I think, head to the cabin not for respite and refuge but for engagement in the struggle.

Bulkington battles mightily against the treacherous winds and storms that he knows threaten to blow him to shore. Lee shores are dangerous to watercraft because, if left to drift, these vessels will be driven onto shore by the wind, and possibly run aground and be destroyed. Indeed, Margaret Fuller drowned off the coast of Fire Island when her ship was blown toward the shore during a hurricane. And Thoreau (2004, 7) says, upon coming across a shipwreck on the shores of Cape Cod, "I was even more surprised at the power of the waves, exhibited on this shattered fragment, than I had been at the sight of the smaller fragments before . . . I saw that no material could withstand the power of the waves." Too close to land, the ship is threatened with destruction. It is better to remain at sea than to approach the Lee Shore. The Lee Shore represents danger because on it one loses the freedom the sea offers.

"Know ye, now, Bulkington?" Ishmael asks. The comma and the appositive reference to the present moment, is significant. It transforms the question that might have been directed toward the reader onto Bulkington as one for whom the land seemed "scorching to his feet" (Melville, 1962,105). Ishmael asserts in the question some identification with Bulkington's appreciation that the Lee Shore means psychological death. Though the question is posed by Ishmael to Bulkington, *Moby Dick* is still Ishmael's memoir, and it is Ishmael's knowledge with which I am concerned foremost here. Ishmael wonders if Bulkington has learned what Ishmael seems to have learned: Bulkington cannot stay ashore, but must continually put out to sea. Though there seems great comfort on the shore, though that shore seems to beckon welcome, it represents a deceptive but dangerous safety.

> Know ye, now, Bulkington? Glimpses do you seem to see of that mortally intolerable truth; that all deep, earnest thinking is but the intrepid effort of the soul to keep the open independence of her sea; while the wildest winds of heaven and earth conspire to cast her on the treacherous, slavish shore?
>
> But as in landlessness alone resides the highest truth, shoreless, indefinite as God—so, better is it to perish in that howling infinite, than be ingloriously dashed upon the lee, even if that were safety! For worm-like, then, oh! who would craven crawl to land! Terrors of the terrible! is all this agony so vain? Take heart, take

heart, O Bulkington! Bear thee grimly, demigod! Up from the spray of thy ocean-perishing—straight up, leaps thy apotheosis!"
(Chapter 23, "The Lee Shore").

Though the shore offers "all that's kind to our mortalities," it is at sea alone where resides "the highest truth, shoreless, indefinite as God." The Lee Shore, that one touch of land, one approach to "safety, comfort, hearthstone, supper, warm blankets, friends," would cause the "ship to shudder through and through." Ashore, in that illusory peace the mythical cabin offers, truth may not be sought or found because it is in struggle and storm that learning and insight may be achieved. In *Moby Dick*, escape is not the goal of the cabin; rather, one inhabits the cabin to engage. "Up from the spray of thy ocean perishing—straight up, leaps thy apotheosis!" Ishmael cries. Only at sea can Bulkington—and Ishmael and, ah and alas, all of us—achieve our highest glory even though the voyage ends in tragedy. The myth of the cabin of escape is a dangerous hoax: the idea of the Pequod as cabin confronts Ishmael and Bulkington with life.

Life is an inconceivable storm, and the winds that would blow us toward the shore threaten our safety. Though we would be in the comfort of our home and amidst all the warmth that there derives, if it is truth we seek then it must be found at sea; we must beware the dangers attendant on the Lee Shore. Better to perish at sea in search of truth than to die upon the lee shore seeking comfort and ease. In the essay "The Pursuit of the Ideal," Berlin writes (2000, 11), "We are doomed to choose, and every choice may entail an irreparable loss. Happy are those who live under a discipline which they accept without question, who freely obey the orders of leaders, spiritual or temporal, whose word is fully accepted as unbreakable law; or those who have, by their own methods, arrived at clear and unshakeable convictions about what to do and what to be that brook no possible doubt. I can only say that those who rest on such uncomfortable beds of dogma are victims of forms of self-induced myopia, blinkers that may make for contentment, but not for understanding of what it is to be human." These souls are neither Bulkington nor Ishmael. Along with these two, I reject the cabin of refuge and transform it into a place of struggle and discovery. In becoming Ishmael, he goes to sea not to retreat from the world but to enter it. Know ye, now, Ishmael, what a glorious and tragic knowledge it is to which you arrive. The Pequod has become, ironically, a cabin, not a place for escape or retreat, but for entrance into struggle and exploration, a place where one might stand before the mast, standing keen and attentive in the mast-head looking for whales.

ME AND THE WHITE WHALE

And what was I doing at the Spouter Inn?

My daughter had enrolled in a class called The Alienated Narrator. I thought that I knew something about alienation and at the moment I had the hypos upon me, and so I chose to follow along with her syllabus and to head out once again on the high seas, read the assigned texts, and engage in the class vicariously through conversations with my daughter on our telephones. One of the earliest texts that I encountered was Melville's great novel, *Moby Dick*. We wondered: If the narrator opens the book with the directive, "Call me Ishmael," then by what other names might he ever have been known? Who was he before he was Ishmael? And why does the narrator assume the name of the outcast brother, Ishmael? What does it mean to be Ishmael? Questions of identity and narration have consumed me for years: "'Shipmates,' Elijah asked, 'have ye shipped in that ship?' 'Yes,' said I, 'we have just signed the articles'" (Melville, 1962, 91). As it happened (or as the Bokononists say, "As it was meant to happen"), Melville's *Moby Dick* exactly suited my frame of mind at that moment, and through Ishmael I signed the articles and I again made the acquaintance of Bulkington; and through Bulkington I came to confront the cabin and the Lee Shore. I considered: for Bulkington and Ishmael the Pequod—well, it seemed that any ship upon the sea would do—served the function of the cabin, but in their occupancy in these spaces it was struggle and not peace they sought. Indeed, only in their struggle would they find their peace. I have shipped aboard several cabins in my life without always knowing that it was struggle I required. From his pulpit in the Whaleman's chapel Father Mapple counseled, "Woe to him who seeks to please rather than to appall! Woe to him whose good name is more to him than goodness! Woe to him who, in this world, courts not dishonor! Woe to him who would not be true, even though to be false were salvation" (47). Out here in this cabin Father Mapple's sermon had been my credo.

This cabin of which I now speak was a bit larger than was Thoreau's home at Walden Pond; measuring fourteen feet by sixteen feet, it sat just beyond the reach of the main house but just before the thick of woods. Named partly after my adoration of Henry David and partly in honor of Zonker's refuge, I referred to the cabin as Walden Puddle. Along its northern, western, and southern walls rested the bookshelves filled in no exact order with a partial stock of the resources and rewards from my academic study. These were my friends out here in my solitude, and I was there to converse, wrestle, labor, and keep company with them. As I circled through that space from early morning until late in the day, I could experience the sun move across the sky from east to west as the light poured into the oversized windows; during the colder months the radiant heat from the floor supplemented the sun's passionate rays and the excellent insulation. This was a clean, well-lighted place. Many (though not all) of my demons were visible.

Lined against the northern, eastern, and southern walls, an array of cluttered desks awaited my attention. A stunning handmade desk sat in the middle of the cabin against the southern wall, framed by the two windows. This piece had been built by a master craftsman from whom I purchased it twenty or so years ago, more for its beauty than for its service. There existed not a nail in the whole piece. It was as much a work of art as it was a serviceable desk. Inside its fold-up top I keep some important papers that could have been stored elsewhere—birth certificates, passports, health reports—a dwindling supply of bank checks, and a stray out of date postal stamp. For the most part I sat here only to study the Torah portions I am regularly assigned for a current Shabbat. Sometimes, buoyed up by that work, I would float on a soft and dirge-like main.

The other desks, facing north, east, and south, are flat-surfaced factory products composed of serviceable but uncertain materials. Atop the desk against the eastern wall rests my computer: it is surrounded inevitably by a stack of books, sheets of papers, piles of writing utensils, post-it notes, coffee cups, and a water bottle. This cluttered array always makes me a bit nervous but I have no facility to make any better order here. It is here I sit (even now) staring intently toward the horizon looking for whales, fighting with what I have already caught, and preparing the catch for storage and then delivery. I tap the case for the valuable precious sperm oil. I take care not to lean too far over: I would not fall into "the very whitest and daintiest of fragrant spermaceti" and die embalmed (343). I consume any number of sweets and cups of coffees and teas. A bit to the right of this desk, standing in the corner behind a five-foot tall photo screen, as a naughty boy stands exiled in a classroom, sits the boiler that heats the water that during the long winter months warms the cabin from beneath the floor. The temperature drops precipitously well before Thanksgiving and I keep several sweaters about to maintain a body temperature suitable for activity.

Sitting before the boiler and to the right of my desk on which sits the computer is a folding screen that hides the unsightly boiler and that displays portraits of my beautiful daughters; a candid snapshot of Bob Dylan given to me by a dear friend who not-so-innocently lifted it from a photo bank where she worked; a photographic print of my grandfather when he was in his youth swinging a tennis racket as if he would ever have been allowed into the Forest Hills Tennis Club that he worshipped; and an eight by ten snapshot of my parents dressed as the tourists they were at the Roman Coliseum back when all of us were younger. I have also set in the screen a portrait of Allan and Helen Mastbaum, the Holocaust survivors who I drove to synagogue every week for five years. Finally, on the screen I have placed two pictures of myself in the classroom taken before my skin creased and my beard turned gray. Once I thought the photo screen would serve as a rotating summary of my life in photographs, but on the one hand I couldn't always remember what those things might be, and on the other hand, I discovered soon that too much effort was required in the making of the exhibits and I abandoned the project. I had other seeds to sow. I preferred to stand in the mast-head and look for whales.

In front of the screen is a clumsy wooden structure—another of the desks—that I had purchased in a thrift store, masquerading as an antique dealer. It is on this desk that faces southeast, but facing nothing but the screen and hidden boiler, that I keep the materials required to attend to my work in the classrooms. The university-issued laptop, course syllabi, and texts litter the surface; inevitably there lies about a folder of papers to be read and commented upon. Along the full base of the desk is a square platform on which I stack more papers and periodicals that I don't know where else to file and cannot bear to discard. Along the northern wall of the cabin another desk looks out on an open field. On it an editor's reading platform sits covered over with soft covered moleskin daybooks into which I distill some products of my thought. Resting on the surface are books—fast fish and loose fish—onto which from the ship I currently cast my gaze. Cookie crumbs lie scattered about the desk's top and the books' bindings.

Finally, facing to the west, contiguous and perpendicular to the north desk, is yet another desk-like surface also cluttered with books and papers. Here sit projects in process, projects planned, and miscellaneous correspondence to which I mean soon to attend. I don't always succeed in doing so.

I recall once reading that Monet would set up a number of easels in the early morning hours and as the light changed he would move from canvas to canvas trying to catch the exact impression of light. On each of the desks in the cabin sit different projects, some fantastical and some quite mundane. Sometimes I think I've organized myself out of the ability to function. Sometimes I move the projects to different desks hoping the change will produce some inspiration. Says Ishmael, "I try all things; I achieve what I can" (Melville, 1962, 343).

Facing west is the door to the cabin: a large glass opening that lets in light and hopefully keeps the darkness out. For the past year or more a nameless black cat regularly and devotedly sits awaiting my entrances and exits and demanding food. I feed him.

On the walls of the cabin are various map-like images that chart phases of my life. Along the eastern (computer) wall are several posters that have traveled with me over the years. Above and just to my left as I write is the poster of Studs Terkel advertising a reading he was doing here in the Twin Cities for his 1995 book *Coming of Age;* and on the right of that window across from Studs and just above eye-level is tacked a twenty-four by thirty-six inch personality poster of Karl Marx that I had purchased in Greenwich Village in 1974 as I became a Marxist, and that hung in my high school English class for almost a decade. Just below Karl Marx, similarly sized hangs a *carefully framed* poster of myself running the last hundred yards or so of the 1983 Philadelphia Marathon. I had had the race photo blown up to poster size and it has been placed conspicuously wherever I have worked; it serves to remind me of what I was once capable even as it taunts me with my ebbing youth.

On the wall to the left of where I sit looking at the computer screen and the woods is a stock photograph of the Western Wall brought to me from Israel by my daughter. Also hanging on that wall is the framed award for the Outstanding Book in 2006 in Division B of AERA, Curriculum Studies, which was given to me for my work *Talmud, Curriculum and The Practical: Joseph Schwab and the Rabbis*. On a metal strip magnets hold a few notices past due, a few dates long passed, and some no longer current memoranda.

On the southern and western walls of the cabin I have hung two more posters of Bob Dylan; on the former a replica of his album *The Times They Are a' Changin'*, and on the latter another personality poster of a baby-faced Dylan in his early twenties, dangling a cigarette in his right hand. Bob Dylan is a major current that runs through the waters of my life. And hanging on the northern wall are various photos and visual reminders of various events—major and minor—in my life: a framed postcard series of Michelangelo's *Il Prigone*, purchased years ago at the *Accademia Galleria* in Florence, a copy of a print by Michelangelo given me during my days of travel by an Italian admirer, a print of Rembrandt's "The Return of the Prodigal Son," and postcard portraits of Thoreau, Whitman, and John Lennon. There is also a three-dimensional art piece by someone named Amrani depicting columns from the *Megillat Esther*. This piece had hung in my parent's home before my father's death and the onset of my mother's dementia. It is what I requested from their home when it was cleared. Around the entrance door to the cabin and surrounding the frame are magnet frames containing pictures of my two beautiful children at various stages of their still young lives.

How did I come to ship aboard this cabin?

For ten years prior, I had worked in the basement of our house in an office I had established in a craggy, dark northeast corner nook. No window broke the expanse of the wall, and no daylight ever entered the space. Attached to the northern wall was an eight-foot counter top desk on which sat my computer and various papers and books relevant to the present project. Behind me, in a narrow alcove no wider than a slightly oversized grave (as say, suitable for a portly Cardinal Wolsey or a massive Queequeg), the walls were lined with my books. Overhead, track lighting illuminated the desk space, and behind me a standing lamp shone on the books. Down to that basement hold I would descend most early mornings followed enthusiastically by the domesticated cats who demanded to be fed their breakfast. Their food bowls and litter boxes were placed in the southeast corner of the full and finished basement, perhaps twenty-five feet behind my workspace. After they had eaten they would relieve themselves before heading back upstairs for their after-meal, early morning nap. They usually and casually left behind the stink of their ordure. Behind me also and in the same corner of the basement as the cats' feeding bowls and litter boxes was the furnace which during the winter would slam on periodically, maintaining the temperature at a comfortable level for those who remained above, but whose workings had little effect in this basement space which I now occupied and certainly disturbed whatever quiet existed down there in the first place. Since heat rises, the basement remained somewhat chilly: during the summertime this was often a boon, but during the darker months required donning a winter sweater. During these colder months, occasionally a little field mouse would scurry along the baseboard perimeter, headed for where it sensed there was sustenance and, where, despite the presence of cats, might reside some safety.

On the other side of the full basement was the area where our laundry was done: an electric washer and dryer that on a good day were empty, but on most days still contained the wash from other days and from which emanated a musty odor. I had once had a great many bookshelves built, and they lined the basement walls filled with more of my treasures. Some of my dearest friends and comrades were these books that sat on these shelves. In my basement office they were my friends and companions. All year, dehumidifiers ran to protect these tomes.

Between the two sides of the basement was a doorless space that contained a toilet, a laundry sink, and a stall shower that no one, not even I, would use save in some dire emergency. Sometimes the clickings and clangings in the basement reminded me of old Jacob Marley's noisy visitation to Ebenezer Scrooge on Christmas Eve. Sometimes I responded exactly as did Scrooge—with horror and dismay—and would symbolically throw the covers over my head and quake. But nevertheless and despite the dank and the noise, early each weekday morning I could descend the stairs into a relative solitude, if not quiet, with a mug of freshly brewed coffee and followed only by the hungry cats. I wrote three books down there. It was, I suppose, an early iteration of the cabin, but then I called it the basement!

In the meantime . . . for years I have read and reread the work of Thoreau whose advocacies I have been trying to live up to for most of my life, and I talked often with whomever would listen about Thoreau's cabin in the woods by the shores of Walden Pond. One day an acquaintance long now gone—who had years ago finished the basement of my home so that I could even go down there to work in the first place—said to me, "Alan, what you need is a Walden Cabin." And for several years after I would fantasize about both the cement Stairway to Heaven I originally wanted to install in my back yard overlooking an empty eighty-acre field, and about my shack, until one day I said, "It is time. If you build it, they will come." And over one summer when I was away in Burlington, Vermont, teaching at a small Catholic college there, a small team of carpenters constructed Walden Puddle (*mea culpa*, Zonker) into which I moved on a warm September morning almost fifteen years ago.

I struggle out here and try to keep from heading toward the Lee Shore. I pace the floor; I gaze out of the windows. I stand alert in the mast-head and look for whales. My cabins have not ever been places for peaceful retreat, and my occupancy in them is not a tranquil one. Though I sometimes nap out here, I do not sleep; though I do not sleep, yet I dream. The allure of my cabin spaces is deceptively inviting but precarious in fact. Nonetheless, I seek them out "especially when my hypos get such an upper hand of me, that it requires a strong moral principle to prevent me from deliberately stepping into the street and methodically knocking people's hats off . . ." (1). It is in my cabins where my thinking "is but the intrepid effort of the soul to keep the open independence of her sea," even while everything blows me toward the shore.

Nathan Zuckerman visits the single room in which Johnny O'Day lives. It, too, is a iteration of the cabin I have been exploring. Zuckerman writes, "Now I understood what Ira was doing in the shack and the stripping back of everything—the aesthetic of the ugly that Eve Frame was to find so insufferable, that left a man lonely and monastic but also unencumbered, free to be bold and unflinching and purposeful. What O'Day's room represented was discipline, that discipline which says that however many desires I have, I can circumscribe myself down to this room. You can risk anything if at the end you know you can tolerate the punishment, and this room was a part of the punishment." This cabin is that room: "[S]o better is it to perish there in that howling infinite, than be ingloriously dashed upon the lee, even if that were safety" (Melville, 1962,105), Ishmael affirms. And the cabin is where I tolerate the punishment that life inflicts. It is here that I do my work. I am an academic. I live at the academy. It is my life work. To a large extent, it is my life. And what work is it that I do here?

Here, I struggle to avoid the Lee Shore; out here I know that all deep, earnest thinking is but the intrepid effort of the soul to keep the open independence of her sea; while the wildest winds of heaven and earth conspire to cast her on the treacherous, slavish shore. Out here, I can tolerate the punishment. I come out here as a means to get away from in there; here, I do things that have become impossible to accomplish in there. Out here, I obsess about things that I have cautioned those in there to let go; I pile up too many books and papers that I will read out here that I have carried from in there. Out here, all seems to maintain perspective. Out here I laugh at what I do, and I despair at what I can't accomplish. At times I lose faith in even that which I have done. Out here, I give admittance to the demons that I close the door to in there, and out here I enjoy some intimations of immortality. "There is nothing like the perils of whaling to breed this free and easy sort of genial, desperado philosophy; and with it I now regarded this whole voyage of the Pequod, and the great White Whale its object" (226). I close the door to the cabin and climb atop the mast-head.

Epilogue: The Classroom as Cabin

The essay's done. What is left to say? I would arise and go now to the schoolrooms in which I have spent almost my entire life. I think now that they are the cabins of which I have spoken and which I have, sometimes unbeknownst to me, sought. These cabins are not the romanticist retreat from the world sought by Worsdworth, Yeats, Dylan, or my neighbors, but more akin to Ishmael's Pequod on which I set sail in my attempt to avoid the Lee Shore. It is hard work but it is honest labor. Ishmael says, "Who ain't a slave. Tell me that . . . however the old sea captains may order me about—however they may thump and punch me about, I have the satisfaction of knowing that it is all right; that everybody else is one or other served in much the same way—either in a physical or metaphysical point of view, that is; and so the universal thump is passed round, and all hands should rub each other's shoulder-blades, and be content" (1962, 4). I arrive on time and leave a bit late. It is in these cabin–classrooms that we occupants clap each others shoulders and give comfort. It is in these cabins that I enact the idea that all deep, earnest thinking is the effort of the soul to maintain the openness and freedom of a life. It is in these cabins that I teach others to stand high atop the deck on the mast and watch dutifully and diligently for whales. It is in these cabins that we encounter our Queequegs and Daggoos, our Starbucks and Stubbs. It is here in our classrooms that we confront our Ahabs. Here we may satisfy our torment for things remote. In these cabins-now become-classrooms we hunt for the white whale.

I am thinking, and it is in the cabin that my thinking best occurs. There it is that I struggle best with the elements. And what needs occur in our classroom-cabins is to "maintain the state of doubt and to carry on systematic and protracted inquiry—these are the essentials of thinking" (Dewey, 1910/1991, 13). As precarious as thinking may be, as attentively as it demands that I stand in the mast-head, all thinking derives from necessary doubt and is, I believe, the essential act of the classroom. This pedagogy of thinking should be the center of curriculum work as we avoid the Lee Shore. Thinking requires that we enter places of conflict and struggle, "to sail forbidden seas, and land on barbarous coasts" (Melville, 1962, 6). Thinking always involves sailing (or marching, as the case may be) out into the wilderness and away from the comfort but danger of the Lee Shore. We ship aboard not knowing exactly where it is we head but certain that we are moving forward. *We* resist, *they* complain, but the good teacher sustains. It is good to have friends and colleagues.

So might such encounter and engagement be the effort of our classroom–cabins. There we engage with the world that we might go out and encounter it; there we encounter the world that we might go out and engage with it. We go to sail forbidden seas and land on barbarous coasts. We are learners. "If a man's actions are not guided by thoughtful conclusions, then they are guided by inconsiderate impulse, unbalanced appetite, caprice, or the circumstance of the moment" (Dewey, 1910/1991, 67). Unreflective thought mires us in the immediate sensory present and leads only to eventual dissatisfaction and no future. And even if someone told me where I could hunt for the whales, would that make capturing them any easier? We transform the classroom into the cabin where we who inhabit it encounter and engage. There we learn to think and the classroom is where we learn to believe.

Know ye, now, Bulkington? I gather my books and my papers and having nothing particular to interest me on shore, I would sail about a little and see the watery part of the world. It is a way I have of driving off the spleen, and regulating the circulation. I would in my sail struggle always to keep from smashing onto the Lee Shore.

Afterword(s)?

William F. Pinar

> Perhaps our complicated conversations are all prefaces—stories of the processes and difficulties in which we engage as we write ourselves.[1]
>
> Alan A. Block

It was a series of prefaces Alan Block had planned to write, "summaries of anticipated adventures." Was anticipation the motive, or was it the experience of the threshold through which one walks to undertake the journey? Perhaps neither, as Block confides to us: "What I had originally thought of as a preface turned out to be more of an afterword." So maybe *this* afterword is a preface, and maybe not only to this work, but to Alan's *oeuvre* overall?[2] No, that preface would take a book and this is an afterword.

Fifteen years ago, understanding education "as the opportunity of getting lost,"[3] Alan Block had abandoned—indeed, he "renounces"[4]—home and even the idea of "path"[5] for the sake of finding the way elsewhere.[6] "The capacity for lostness," Block insisted, "is the beginning of educative experience."[7] What takes us there, to the land where one becomes lost and undergoes educational experience? It is "books," he tells us; they "send me out from my native land to the land that they might show me."

Anticipation may remain as one reads (and writes)[8] but it appears to be anticipation emptied of expectation concerning the specificity of destination,[9] as, he emphasizes, "I *shouldn't* know exactly where I was going if I were going to learn anything along the way: I couldn't write a preface until the end of the journey. But I had taken no journey; I couldn't write a preface." Anticipation doesn't disappear but here the reflective gaze turns backward, toward the past not the future: "What I had originally thought of as a preface turned out to be more of an afterword." I had imagined these prefaces were beginnings, but now, I realize, they are the end. This afterword is, perhaps, both.

No self-pity: looking back provides opportunities for the acknowledgment of blessings. In the 1387 Christian definition of 'preface' (that Alan quotes) that was indeed the practice; it was, he explains, an "exhortation to thanksgiving." For Jews, the *P'sukei d'zimrah* serves as a "preface": "prayers of praise that precede the formal service." For both traditions, Block notes, "a preface serves as preparation for the main event." Anticipation becomes prolonged—indeed institutionalized—through ritual. Even an afterword prepares one for the main event, an event that occurs in part within the reader. Perhaps the afterword is the "afterlife" of the work.[10]

"The chapters that follow," Block prepares us, "represent some of the markers at which I have paused for various amounts of reason and time throughout my life, but from which for any number of reasons and time I have also moved." They are "autobiographies in disguise," he adds. "For Thoreau, as for Montaigne, Adams, and Roth, our responsibility in this life is to know our selves, and I believe that that knowledge includes a keen and critical awareness of our place in the world."[11] That place is material, historical,[12] subjective,[13] and always relational. "Reading engages us in relationships," Block understands, "and we are always changed by these intimacies."[14] Perhaps we learn from them, but as we "read" the relationships in which we are embedded, we learn what we had not anticipated. We enjoy *educational* experience.[15] "When we read we find something we did not know to look for because we had not known it had been even lost." By being lost we can find our place: "My readings send me out into the world," Block recounts, and in so doing "my imagination grows and my reality deepens." There is almost a dialectic here: "To the books I bring the life I have lived and thought, and it is from these books that I go back changed to the world of reality." For Block, that world is also temporal, and the imagination we need is a prophetic one.[16]

THE QUESTION MY LIFE PRESENTS

> To speak to another is to hear that other's voice in the form of a question or a demand addressed to me.
>
> Block (2007, 69)

"What I am interested in at present," Block confides, "is the manner and motives of those who *do* read and who *choose* the books to be read. And I believe that the answer to this query remains a question: we choose our reading to answer a question that has been posed to us." This is probably no ordinary question, as it is one that in fact structures one's entire life: "I choose my reading by the question my life presents to me about my existence, and from my reading I seek some response." That question is not always audible, and so one keeps reading, hoping not only for an answer but to hear the question.

One day after class—a class during which Professor Block's questions go unanswered—a student named Hannah asks him about Hemingway's *The Sun Also Rises*, wondering if he knew what the point of it is. Was she also asking about the readings in the class? Was she searching for a bridge to her professor's world, a world she couldn't comprehend? Or was she expressing what she has been trained to ask: What's the answer to the test question?

No longer "an open activity engaged in for its own sake," Block laments, "reading is performed in order to 'get the point' so that some question posed by some authority might be correctly answered."

One way to understand this book—Block shifts from Hemingway to himself—is to regard "writing" as an "open activity," to be "engaged in for its own sake." In an age of instrumentalism[17]—where activity is reduced to a means to an end—affirming the intrinsic significance of study (including reading and writing) constitutes progressive education.[18]

"Have we organized education," Block asks (knowing the answer), "so that students only proffer answers rather than ask questions?" To Hannah, you recall, Professor Block pauses, then replies: "Hannah, perhaps the book doesn't have a point." Perhaps the book itself is a question. After all, "a question is . . . the beginning of knowledge." In our Weimar time, knowledge not 'skills', questions not answers, subjective presence not virtual Internet identity become markers of progressive education. Lost, the question is not: What's the point? The question concerns place and time: Where are we? What time is it?

The Curriculum Question

> I think we must be careful of the questions we pose each other, and the questions to which we demand response.
>
> Alan A. Block (2010, 525)

Where we are, Block knows, is in "a society that is not interested in questions." Moreover, "we have come as a society to expect and to value only the answer into which we have placed all of our faith, and have reserved little respect for the unanswerable question." The unanswerable question—it is simultaneously spiritual, subjective, political, and educational—is the curriculum question: What knowledge is most worth? Posing that question keeps us attuned to time and place, including the past[19] where the future lies buried.

Wandering in the desert[20]—lost, timeless—requires keeping the faith, and in a secular age the medium of faith is the imagination. Block knows: "I am driven to the book by not knowing, for though I know I cannot know, I can imagine. To imagine is why I read." This is not imagination only as occasion for creativity or fantasy, this is the medium of religious experience: "Reading and writing stretches me to the limits of my consciousness." As theorizing was for James B. Macdonald, study—reading and writing—is for Alan Block a form of prayer.[21]

Prayer plays a primary role in Block's thought, ritualizing the anticipation embedded in "study,"[22] restructuring education as reverential, as acknowledgment of being lost, alone[23] and together.[24] "Study is," Block explains, "a stance we assume in the world . . . Study offers us moments of insight and chances for direction." Study is not test preparation but meditation, not a means but an end. "Study emanates from the silence of awe and wonder." It may sound like we're in a church or synagogue, but actually we're in "school."

Not school deformed by "reform," this school is a place for study. Its classrooms may not look like classrooms; they could be cabins. "The ideal cabin came to serve as the escape from the reality of the library and laboratory," Block reports. It could become a place "where original, unmediated experience might be enjoyed." Such a place is perhaps metaphoric: "As much as they are physical places, cabins and shacks seem to be psychological spaces, locations that occur as much *in the mind* as in the actual world." For Virginia Woolf, Alan reminds us, that cabin was a room of one's own. But this place of promise prompts a caution, and Alan asks: "What if the imagined retreat into the cabin was nothing more than a dangerous delusion?" He admits: "My cabins have not ever been places for peaceful retreat, and my occupancy in them is not a tranquil one." So maybe not a place for meditation, but rather, one for thinking?[25] "I am thinking, and it is in the cabin that my thinking best occurs." In fact, Block says, echoing Melville's Ishmael, "It is in these cabins that I enact the idea that all deep, earnest thinking is the effort of the soul to maintain the openness and freedom of a life."

That is the question, is it not, "the effort of the soul to maintain the openness and freedom of a life"? For *that* effort, what knowledge is of most worth? That is the question that keeps us open, attuned to the historical moment, aware we are lost, anticipating what we don't yet know we even want. It is the question of study. "There is nothing beyond the answer," Alan Block reminds, "but by the question the world is open to possibility." In such a curriculum teaching becomes "prophecy." Alan Block's teaching is such prophecy, as this preface testifies, afterward.

Notes

1. Unless otherwise indicated, all quoted passages are from this volume.
2. In terms of books—and there are many articles (including a groundbreaking exposition of study [2001]) and book chapters (including a superb study of Maxine Greene [1998a])—Block starts from Marxism with his subtle and insightful study of the radical novel in twentieth-century America. He moves to reading—working with Frank Smith, Jeanne Chall, and other key figures—which he reconceptualizes through Dewey, James, and concludes memorably with "three readers reading." Next came an unexpected psychoanalytic turn (1997), not with clinical coldness but heartfelt fear, including (I suspect) for his school-aged daughters. The "religious" turn followed. First he stripped Schwab clean of simplicity (2004), contextualizing that canonical work in Judaism, turning afterward to Torah study to rethink American—indeed Western—education (2007, 2009). It is scale and sophistication of scholarly achievement few can claim and by which the field is forever enriched.
3. Block 1998b, 328.

4. Block 1998b, 329.
5. Block 1998b, 330.
6. "Thoreau notes," Block (1998b, 330) reminds us (quoting his alter ego), "how quickly the single path he had worn to the pond for his morning ablutions supervised and determined his way, and how he then knew how that he would have to leave Walden, for 'I had other lives to live'." From there he moves into Marxism (1998b, 333–335) from which it seems, for a while, there is nowhere to go until he returns to being lost and the creative expressivity it offers, referencing the "dadaists, the affichistes, the collages of Robert Rauchenberg and Richard Hamilton, and the graffiti artists of the 1980s" (Block 1998b, 336).
7. Block 1997, 119.
8. "Writing always denies home and paths," Block (1998b, 331) believes, "because to write is to understand that meaning is situationally dependent."
9. "The presence of objectives," Block knows (this volume), "suggested that there should be no adventure in education. In fact, I thought, objectives obstructed the educational journey rather than facilitated it: they kept asleep the curiosity so essential to learning."
10. This is an idea associated with Walter Benjamin (whose work Alan quotes in several places over the years: see, for instance, 1992, 122; 1995, 118). To situate the concept in Benjamin's life, see Eiland and Jennings 2014, 109, 158.
11. "As did Marx from the other side of the world," Block writes, "Thoreau argued that most importantly we must own ourselves, and that this accomplishment derives from a self-knowledge that might prevent a life of servitude and quiet desperation. Men may make their own history, but not in the circumstances of their choosing: we must learn our circumstances to understand our freedom." Put another way, as Alan does in chapter 2, "reality does not rupture my imagination but comes to substance through it."
12. "[U]ntil the historical [becomes] personal," Block writes, one has "no idea where [one] is." History doesn't disappear into autobiography, but by entering History that past does become personal. "To understand the word," Alan suggests, "one must always go into

the past. And sometimes, that past is not even my past!" In an age of presentism, the past provides a place of momentary escape, a "cabin" where "thinking" might occur. "Unreflective thought," Block warns, "mires us in the immediate sensory present and leads only to eventual dissatisfaction and no future." Presentism is not being in the present moment but absent from it.

13. "I would prefer to replace the notion of subjectivity with the idea of identity," Block (1998b, 332) admits, affirming relationality and materiality. In this volume he focuses on "the complex codes . . . that bound my life." The "lost book" might "afford [him] precious insights" into these codes, and, he tells us, "I read regularly to find this book."

14. Those intimacies can originate in family, as they evidently did for Alan: "My mother used to adore telling others how I would run to her (to *her,* of course!) with a book held out in my hands and cry, 'Read to me, read to me!' I cannot say what led me to books in the first place, though I now suspect that it was the opportunity to be held in her lap whilst she read. Perhaps books were the means to receive warmth and attention." It would seem so, as in another place in this volume Alan confides: "I loved reading with my daughters—I love reading." When leaving home does one retain—through reading—the sense of intimacy associated with the family? "I read somewhere that the book written is meant to repair the rift that exists between the word and the world," Block remembers.

15. "The purpose of [reading]," Block (1995, 103) reminds us, "is the production of meaning."

16. "We are in schools," Block (2007, 199) writes, "much in need of the prophetic imagination: perhaps it is the prophetic tradition to which teachers might adhere rather than to that of the statisticians." Statisticians reduce children's learning to scores on standardized tests. School 'reform' is not about learning but about "control" and "mastery," as Thorndike was unafraid to say straight out in 1913: "Tables of correlation seem dull, dry, unimpressive things besides the insights of poets and proverb-makers—but only to those who miss their meaning. In the end they will contribute tenfold more to man's mastery of himself" (quoted in Block 1995, 95). "Control," Block (2007, 77) laments, "that is the only answer in the classrooms of the United States."

17. "We have assumed an instrumentalist stand," Block knows.
18. Historical context construes conceptualization. In an age of recitation and memorization, the early-twentieth-century emphasis on projects, skills, process were in fact "progressive." In an age where students know nothing except how to do what they're told—to find "answers" as Block puts it—then "knowledge" becomes of intrinsic importance. What had been "traditional" a century ago is now "progressive." As Block (1992, 20) notes in his study of the American radical novel, "radicalism . . . is a product of a particular historical context and that the form of that radicalism—and its production in and as literature—alters with changing conditions and not with particular parties. In an age of stupidity, preserving the past—once the definition of conservatism—becomes progressive: "To teachers is given the almost religious task of guarding and fostering intelligence."
19. The "past" is not only what we remember—History—it is, Block (2009, 67) notes, also what we don't: "I think we are always burdened by the past that we don't remember."
20. "Education is our means out of the desert," Block (2009, 111) affirms. "While we study, there is no desert. And this study built upon faith is the substance of curriculum."
21. See Macdonald 1995. Block (2004, 2): "Study, I aver, is a prayerful act."
22. Part of the problem of the present is that "study ha[s] become secular and not sacred. Study ha[s] lost its base in wonder and awe and ha[s] become mundane." It is about 'measurement.' (In his study of reading, Block [1995, 95] quotes William James: "Never were as many men of a decidedly empiricist proclivity in existence as there are at the present day . . . our esteem for facts has not neutralized in us all religiousness. It is itself almost religious. Our scientific temper is devout." Add technology and profit-at-any-cost to this religious faith in 'evidence' and welcome to the twenty-first century, also, like James' time, a "Gilded America.") For the Rabbis, Block reminds us, "study is not merely an essential and practical enterprise but rather, is a holy one."
23. "Thoreau," Block (2009, 47) points out, "lived a life of solitariness amidst great sociability . . . He decries the current insistence on society and sociability, finding too much company distracting."

24. In fact, relationship can be primary. "But for Yohanan and Lakish," Block (2007, 181) explains, "education had been a relationship and the acquisition of knowledge as participation."
25. "This pedagogy of thinking," Block argues, "should be the center of curriculum work."

References

Block, Alan. 1992. *Anonymous Toil: A Re-evaluation of the American Radical Novel in the Twentieth Century*. Lanham, MD: University Press of America.

Block, Alan. 1995. *Occupied Reading*. New York: Garland.

Block, Alan A. 1997. *I'm Only Bleeding: Education as the Practice of Social Violence against the Child*. New York: Peter Lang.

Block, Alan A. 1998a. "'And He Pretended to Be a Stranger to Them. . . .' Maxine Greene and Teacher as Stranger." In *The Passionate Mind of Maxine Greene*, edited by William F. Pinar (14–29). London: Falmer.

Block, Alan A. 1998b. "Curriculum as Affichiste: Popular Culture and Identity." In *Curriculum: Toward New Identities*, edited by William F. Pinar (325–341). New York: Garland.

Block, Alan A. 2001. "Ethics and Curriculum." *JCT* 17 (3), 23–38.

Block, Alan A. 2004. *Talmud, Curriculum, and the Practical*. New York: Peter Lang.

Block, Alan A. 2007. *Pedagogy, Religion, and Practice: Reflections on Ethics and Teaching*. New York: Palgrave Macmillan.

Block, Alan A. 2009. *Ethics and Teaching: A Religious Perspective on Revitalizing Education*. New York: Palgrave Macmillan.

Block, Alan A. 2010. "And They'll Say That It's a Movement." In *Curriculum Studies Handbook: The Next Moment*, edited by Erik Malewski (523–527). New York: Routledge.

Eiland, Howard and Jennings, Michael W. 2014. *Walter Benjamin. A Critical Life*. Cambridge, MA: Belknap Press of Harvard University Press.

Macdonald, Bradley J. Ed. 1995. *Theory as a Prayerful Act: The Collected Essays of James B. Macdonald*. (Introduction by William F. Pinar). New York: Peter Lang.

Bibliography

Adams, H. (1961). *The Education of Henry Adams*. Boston: Houghton-Mifflin.
Agnon, S. (1995). *The Book That Was Lost and Other Stories* (A. Mintz and G. Hoffman, Eds., and A. Gurt, Trans.). New York: Schocken.
Austen, J. (2004). *Mansfield Park*. New York: Barnes & Noble.
Auster, P. (2012). *Winter Journal*. New York: Henry Holt.
Beckett, S. (1954). *Waiting for Godot*. New York: Grove.
Berger, J. (2011). *Bento's Sketchbook: How does the Impulse to Draw Something Begin?* New York: Pantheon.
Berlin, I. (2000). *The Proper Study of Mankind*. New York: Farrar, Straus & Giroux.
Berlin, I. (2013). *Against the Current* (H. Hardy, Ed.). Princeton, NJ: Princeton University Press.
Berlin, I. (2013). *Against the Current*. Princeton, NJ: Princeton University Press.
Block, A. A. (1994). *Occupied Reading*. New York: Garland.
Block, A. A. (2004). *Talmud, Curriculum and the Practical: Joseph Schwab and the Rabbis*. New York: Peter Lang.
Block, A. A. (2009). *Ethics and Teaching*. New York: Palgrave-Macmillan.
Britzman, D. (2003). *Practice Makes Practice*. Albany: SUNY Press.
Buber, M. (1991). *Tales of the Hasidim*. New York: Schocken Press.
Camus, A. (1972). *The Plague* (S. Gilbert, Trans.). New York: Vintage.
Dewey, J. (1893). *Christianity and Democracy. Religious Thought at the University of Michigan*, 60–69. Ann Arbor, MI: Register Publishing Co., Inland Press.

Dewey, J. (1910/1991). *How We Think*. Buffalo, NY: Prometheus.
Eagleton, T. (1996). *The Illusions of Postmodernism*. Oxford: Blackwell.
Eagleton, T. (2012). *The Event of Literature*. New Haven: Yale University Press.
Erskine, J. (1915). *The Moral Responsibility to be Intelligent and Other Essays*. New York: Duffield and Company.
Gallop Poll; http://pdkintl.org/wp-content/blogs.dir/5/files/2012-Gallup-poll-full-report.pdf
Hampl, P. (1999). *I Could Tell You Stories: Sojourns in the Land of Memory*. New York: W.W. Norton.
Heschel, A. J. (1959). *Between God and Man: An Interpretation of Judaism* (F. A. Rothschild, Ed.). New York: Free Press.
Heschel, A. J. (1962). *The Prophets, Volume I*. New York: Harper & Row.
James, W. (1892/1961). *Psychology: The Briefer Course* (G. Allport, Ed.). Notre Dame, IN: University of Notre Dame Press.
James, W. (1962). *Talks to Teachers and to Students on Some of Life's Ideals*. Mineola, NY: Dover.
Labaree, D. (Summer, 2010). "Targeting Teachers." *Dissent*.
Leeser, W. (1993). *Hiding in Plain Sight: Essays in Criticism and Autobiography*. San Francisco: Mercury House.
Levinas, E. (1990). *Difficult Freedom: Essays on Judaism*. (S. Hand, Trans.). Baltimore: Johns Hopkins University.
Mangiel, A. (1996). *The History of Reading*. New York: Viking.
Melville, H. (1962). *Moby Dick*. New York: Hendricks House.
Milosz, C. (1981). *The Captive Mind* (J. Zielonko, Trans.). New York: Vintage International.
Milosz, C. (1968). *Native Realm: A Search for Self-Definition* (C. S. Leach, Trans.). New York: Farrar, Straus & Giroux.
Montaigne, M. d. (2003). *The Complete Works* (D. M. Frame, Trans.). New York: Alfred A. Knopf.
Olson, S. (1997). *Listening Point*. Minneapolis, MN: University of Minnesota Press.
Pirsig, R. (2006). *Zen and the Art of Motorcycle Maintenance*. New York: Harper/Torch.
Ravitch, D. (2010). *The Death and Life of the Great American School System*. New York: Basic Books.

Ravitch, D. (2013). *Reign of Error: The Hoax of the Privatization Movement and the Danger to America's Public Schools*. New York: Alfred A. Knopf.
Robinson, M. (2004). *Gilead*. New York: Picador.
Roth, P. (1988). *The Facts: A Novelist's Autobiography*. New York: Penguin.
Roth, P. (1996). *American Pastoral*. New York: Houghton-Mifflin.
Roth, P. (1998). *I Married a Communist*. New York: Houghton-Mifflin.
Roth, P. (2000). *The Human Stain*. New York: Houghton-Mifflin.
Roth, P. (2010). *Nemesis*. New York: Houghton Mifflin Harcourt.
Rushdie, S. (2012). *Joseph Anton*. New York: Random House.
Seneca (2004). *Letters from a Stoic* (R. Cambell, Trans.). New York: Penguin Classics.
Spinoza, B. d. (1955). *On the Improvement of the Understanding; The Ethics; Correspondence* (R. Elwes, Trans.). New York: Dover.
Sterne, L. (1980). *Tristram Shandy*. New York: W.W. Norton.
Thoreau, H. D. (1960). *Walden*. New York: Signet.
Thoreau, H. D. (1961). *A Week on the Concord and Merrimack Rivers*. New York: Thomas Y. Crowell.
Thoreau, H. D. (2001). *Collected Essays and Poems*. New York: Library of America.
Thoreau, H. D. (2004). *Cape Cod* (J. J. Moldenhauer, Ed.). Princeton, NJ: Princeton University Press.
Tolstoy, L. (2007). *War and Peace* (R. A. Pevear, Trans.). New York: Vintage.
Thrall, William Flint and Hibbard, Addison. (1960). *A Handbook to Literature*. New York: The Odyssey Press.
Trilling, L. (2000). *The Moral Obligation to be Intelligent* (L. Wieseltier, Ed.). New York: Farrar, Straus and Giroux.
Trollope, Anthony. (1857/2005), *Barchester Towers*. New York: Barnes and Noble.
Updike, J. (1963). *The Centaur*. New York: Fawcett.
Vico, G. (1990). *On the Study Methods of Our Time* (E. Gianturco, Trans.). Ithaca, NY: Cornell University Press.
Walton, K. (1990). *Mimesis as Make Believe: On the Foundations of the Representational Arts*. Cambridge, MA: Harvard University Press.

Weinberg, S. (7 November 2013). "Physics: What We Do and Don't Know." *New York Review of Books.*
Westbrook, R. (1991). *John Dewey and American Democracy.* Ithaca, NY: Cornell University Press.
Winterson, J. (1985). *Oranges are Not the Only Fruit.* New York: Grove.
Winterson, J. (2011). *Why Be Happy When You Can Be Normal.* New York: Grove.
Woolf, V. (2005). *A Room of One's Own.* New York: Harvest.

Index

accountability 93
Adams, Henry 13, 15–16, 18, 172
Addams, Jane 53
Adventures of Huckleberry Finn
   (Twain) 61, 146
affichistes 177n6
Agnon, Shmuel Yosef 38, 40
agoraphobia 134
Alito, Samuel 73
ambiguity 94, 96, 119, 135
American Pastoral (Roth) 95
assessments 68, 93, 95–6
   see also common core standards
Austen, Jane 146
Auster, Paul 34, 36–7
autobiography 12–16, 29, 33, 36,
   38, 62, 104, 138, 142, 174,
   177n12
awe 72, 91–3, 148, 155, 175,
   179n22

Barchester Towers (Trollope) 7
Bartleby the Scrivener
   (Melville) 96
Beckett, Samuel 98
being right 94–5
benevolence 72, 97–8, 101
Benjamin, Walter 177n10
Bennett, William 97
Berger, John 24

Berlin, Isaiah 34, 38, 58–61, 93,
   140, 142, 158
Bloomberg, Michael 97
Bobbitt, Franklin 53
Book of Deuteronomy 17
Book of Exodus 17
Book of Jeremiah 71
Book of Micah 97
"Book That Was Lost, The"
   (Agnon) 38–41
books
   character and 21–2
   choosing 28–33
   codes and 43–5
   education and 30–1
   emotion and 36–8
   imagination and 28, 35
   importance of 22–5
   perspective and 45–9
   prefaces and 1–7, 10–19
Britzman, D. 54
Brown v. Board of Education 42
Bulkington 151, 154–60, 170
Bush, George W. 97

cabins, as refuge
   Austen, Jane and 146
   author and 129–35, 159–68
   Berlin, Isaiah and 140, 142
   classroom as cabin 168–70

cabins, as refuge—*Continued*
   Dylan, Bob and 145–6
   escape and 136–7
   Huckleberry Finn and 146
   Judeo-Christian culture
      and 138
   Moby Dick and 150–9
   mythical nature of 137, 142
   Olson, Sigurd and 138, 147–8, 153
   Romantics and 142–3
   Roth, Philip and 148–50
   Thoreau and 137–8, 141, 146–8
   Vico, Giambattista and 140
   Woolf, Virginia and 147
   Wordsworth, William
      and 138–41, 143, 146
   Yeats, William Butler and 145–7, 153
Canterbury Tales, The (Chaucer) 11
Caro, Joseph 39
Carter, Sydney 87
Centaur, The (Updike)
   George Caldwell 52–4, 59–60, 113–27
   knowledge and 113
   overview 51–3
   portrayal of teachers 53–4, 59–61
   study of 54–6, 64
Chall, Jeanne 176n2
charity 112, 146
Chaucer, Geoffrey 5, 10–11
childhood 143–5, 150
Christmas Carol, A (Dickens) 166
classroom
   accountability and 68–9, 93
   aim/objectives and 2–3, 17
   assessment and 95–6
   cabins and 161–2, 168–70
   Centaur and 115–20, 125–6
   concepts of 53–5, 69
   engaging students 2–3, 55–7, 98
   I Married a Communist
      and 104, 106, 110
   Joan of Arcadia and 73–4, 76, 81–3, 86
   knowledge and 90
   prefaces and 9–10
   Socrates and 63
   teachers' responsibility and 69, 90, 98–9
   "the point" and 57, 62–3
Coates, J. B. 135
codes, societal 41–4
Coming of Age (Terkel) 171
common core standards 68, 90, 93, 96
   see also assessments
conceptualization 179n19
contextualization 53, 176n2
Counts, George 53, 104
Cox, Perry 94, 97, 99
critical thinking 43, 58, 107
criticism 31, 36, 140
curiosity 3, 25, 29, 66, 72, 92, 177n9
currere 104
curricula 42, 100, 108, 113–14, 164, 169, 174–6

Dadaism 177n6
democracy 67, 111–12
Desire 16–17, 24–5, 29–33
destiny 134, 142
Dewey, John 3, 10, 53, 70, 84, 95, 104, 110–12, 169–70, 176n2

Index

Dickinson, Emily 31
Duncan, Arne 97
Dylan, Bob 3–4, 25, 136, 145–6, 162, 164, 168
Dylan, Reb 97

education
  Adams, Henry and 13–15
  aim of 2–3
  criticism and 31
  Dewey, John and 70
  effectiveness of 68–70
  Erskine, John and 69–70
  intelligence and 70–2
  pedagogy 59, 62
  philosophy of 53–4, 62–3, 65
  preface and 6, 19
  public policy and 67–9
  rabbis and 71–2
  reading and 31–2, 51, 59
  Socratic method and 58
  study and 71–3
Educational Teacher Preparation Assessment (edTPA) 68, 90
Eliot, George 31
Emerson, Ralph Waldo 13
endings 7–9
Enlightenment 139, 143, 147
Erskine, John 69
Ethan Frome (Wharton) 31
Ethics and Teaching (Block) 54
etymologies 154

Facts: A Novelist's Autobiography (Roth) 15, 36
faith 113, 119, 127, 135, 141, 143–4, 174–5
freedom 111–12, 126, 141–2, 147, 153, 169, 176
Frost, Robert 19, 37

Ginsburg, Ruth Bader 73
Greene, Maxine 176n2

Hamilton, Richard 177n6
Hamlet (Shakespeare) 13, 25, 95
Hampl, Patricia 38
Hannah (student) 56–7, 61–4, 66, 173–4
"Hedgehog and the Fox, The" (Berlin) 34
Hemingway, Ernest 56, 64, 173–4
Heschel, Abraham Joshua 91–2, 112
Hibbard, Addison 5
Hirsch, E. D. 97
history
  codes and 41–2
  knowledge and 76–86, 140
  Judaism and 39
  Tolstoy's theory of 34
Holden Caulfield (*The Catcher in the Rye*) 24
Human Stain, The (Roth) 35
Hundred Years' War (1337–1453) 73, 75, 78–9, 82, 84
hunger 69
Hunter, Madelyn 97
Hutchins, Robert 53

I Married a Communist (Milosz) 101–13, 148
Il Prigone (Michelangelo) 164
immortality 144, 168
in media res 6, 8, 15
innocence 9, 141, 143, 150
Intimations Ode (Wordsworth) 143–4
Ishmael (*Moby Dick*)
  see *Moby Dick*

Index

Jacobi, Friedrich Heinrich   142
James, Henry   11
James, William   70, 106–7, 176n2, 179n22
Joan of Arc   73, 75
Joan of Arcadia (TV show)   72–86
Jonah   138
Joseph Anton: A Memoir (Rushdie)   34
Judaism   4–5, 26–7, 38–9, 71–2, 96–7, 172, 179n22
   see also Torah
Julian of Norwich   87

King and I, The   38
King Henry V   73
King Solomon   87–8
Klein, Joel   97

Labaree, David   54, 99
Lake Champlain   129, 134
Leaves of Grass (Whitman)   11, 13
Lee Shore   65, 135, 156–8, 160, 167–70
Leeser, Wendy   12
Lennon, John   164
Levinas, Emmanuel   79
Listening Point   148
literacy   32

Macdonald, James B.   175
Mansfield Park (Austen)   146
Mao Zedong   131–2
Marx, Karl   18, 131–2, 171, 176n2, 177n6
McCarthyism   102, 104
Melville, Herman   24, 96, 150–1, 157, 159, 163, 167, 169, 176
memory   23, 34, 37, 46–9, 105, 107

Michelangelo   164
Milosz, Czeslaw   12, 34–5, 38, 90, 100–1
"Mississippi" (Dylan)   3–4
Moby Dick (Melville), as memoir
   Bulkington   151, 154–60
   cabins and   150–9, 167–8
   escape and   150–3
   identity and   159–60
   "Loomings,"   152–4
   "Mast-Head,"   150–2
   peace and   152–4
   Pip   24
Monet, Claude   45, 171
Montaigne, Michel de   14–18, 172
Moral Obligation to Be Intelligent (Erskine)   69
morality   31, 60, 71, 102, 105–6, 112, 117, 124, 126–7, 140, 152, 167
"Morality of Inertia, The" (Trilling)   31
"My Pedagogic Creed" (Dewey)   110–11

Narcissus   152
Nation at Risk report   68, 89
National Council for the Accreditation of Teacher Education (NCATE)   90
Native Realm (Milosz)   12, 34
Nature   138–43, 146, 150
Nemesis (Roth)   25–8
Newark, New Jersey   26, 102, 108
"Not Dark Yet" (Dylan)   136

objectives   2–3, 10, 17, 92, 94–5, 177n9
Observation and Appraisal Management System (OASYS)   68

INDEX

Occupied Reading (Block) 32
Olson, Sigurd 138, 147–8, 153
On the Study of Methods of Our Time (Vico) 58
Oranges are Not the Only Fruit (Winterson) 37
Other 38, 124
Oxford English Dictionary (OED) 4–5, 11

physics 91, 95
Pirsig, Robert 63
poverty 39, 41, 59, 69
preface, meaning of 4–6
Prelude, The (Wordsworth) 138–40
present 23, 37–8, 49, 76, 81, 84, 170, 178n12
Pride and Prejudice (Austen) 46–7
P'sukei d'zimrah 4–5, 172
public policy 67
public schools 32, 67–8, 89, 102
"Pursuit of the Ideal" (Berlin) 158

rabbis
 see Judaism
radicalism 179n18
Rauchenberg, Robert 177n6
Rav Yehudah 72
Ravitch, Diane 70, 97
Reason 58, 90, 140–3
Rembrandt 164
responsibility 3, 18, 25, 67–9, 102, 105, 124–5, 138, 172
rhetoric 67–8, 100
Romanticism 140, 142–3, 145
Rosencrantz and Guildenstern are Dead (Stoppard) 127n1

Roth, Philip 15–16, 18, 25, 35–6, 38, 95, 97, 101–2, 107–9, 148–9, 172
Rousseau, Jean-Jacques 142
Rushdie, Salman 34

sacred 4–5, 72–4, 84, 111, 179n22
salvation 112, 125, 160
Sanhedrin 96
Schwab, Joseph 164, 176n2
Scrubs (TV show) 94, 97–9
secular 4, 72, 111, 175
self-deprecation 122, 124
self-expression 142
self-knowledge 17–18, 30, 177n11
Seneca 25, 88
sensory present 170, 178n12
"Sign on the Window" (Dylan) 145
silence 36, 38, 55, 62, 89, 92, 118, 148, 175
simplicity 137, 141, 145, 148–9, 176n2
Sisyphus 55, 57
Smith, Frank 176n2
social order 41, 110–11
Socrates 58, 63
Spinoza, Benedictus de 37, 112
standardized testing 61, 64, 69, 90, 92–3, 98, 108, 178n16
 see also test scores
statistics 67, 178n16
Sterne, Laurence 8
stoicism 25, 88
Stoppard, Tom 127n1
subjectivity 178n13
Sun Also Rises, The (Hemingway) 56–7, 63–4, 66, 173

Talmud, Curriculum and The Practical: Joseph Schwab and the Rabbis (Block)   164
"Targeting Teachers" (Labaree)   54
teaching
 critical thinking and   107
 current state of   92–3
 democracy and   111–12
 Dewey, John and   110–12
 heroic nature of   100–1, 113
 Heschel, Abraham Joshua and   112
 idealization of   94
 impossible nature of   112
 James, William and   106–7
 knowledge and   90–2
 public perception of   89–90, 96
 responsibilities of   98–100
 risks/difficulties of   94–6
 Roth, Philip and   101–10, 112
 rules/regulations and   90, 94
 stoicism and   87–9
 Updike, John and   113–27
 waiting and   96–8
Terkel, Studs   171
test scores   10, 69, 178n16
 see also standardized testing
Thoreau, Henry David
 cabins and   137–8, 141, 146–8, 153, 156, 160
 influence on author   166
 knowledge and   17–18
 on routine   134
 on shipwreck   157
 on simplicity   137
 prefaces and   11
 reading and   32, 48
 self-awareness and   17–18, 172, 177n11
 society and   179n23
 uncertainty and   94–5
 wonder and   90–2
 see also Walden
Thrall, William Flint   5
Times They Are a' Changin', The (Dylan)   164
Tolstoy, Leo   34–5, 37
Torah   71–2, 76, 161, 176n2
 see also Judaism
Trilling, Lionel   31
Tristram Shandy (Sterne)   8
Trollope, Anthony   7–8
truth   35–7, 58–62, 67–8, 111, 115, 141, 157–8
Tyler, Ralph   97

uncertainty   2, 94, 96, 99, 109, 113
unions   89, 101
Updike, John   51, 54–5, 61, 113, 117, 121–2, 124–7

value added   69
Vico, Giambattista   58–60, 62, 140
violence   69, 79, 81

Waiting for Godot (Beckett)   88, 98
Walden (Thoreau)   11, 17–18, 48, 129, 146, 148, 160, 166, 177n6
Walton, Kendall   60, 72
War and Peace (Tolstoy)   34
Weinberg, Steven   91, 95
Westbrook, Robert   111
Wharton, Edith   31
Whitman, Walt   11, 13, 21, 164

Why Be Normal When You Can Be Happy? (Winterson)   33
Wilde, Oscar   48–9
Winterson, Jeanette   23–4, 33–4, 36–8, 44
wonder   72, 91–2, 148, 154, 179n22
Woolf, Virginia   147, 175
Wordsworth, William   138–41, 143, 146, 153

"World is too Much With Us" (Wordsworth)   138
writing   10–18, 24, 37–8, 174–5

Yeats, William Butler   145–7, 153, 168

Zen and the Art of Motorcycle Madness (Pirsig)   63
Zeus   55

GPSR Compliance
The European Union's (EU) General Product Safety Regulation (GPSR) is a set of rules that requires consumer products to be safe and our obligations to ensure this.

If you have any concerns about our products, you can contact us on

ProductSafety@springernature.com

In case Publisher is established outside the EU, the EU authorized representative is:

Springer Nature Customer Service Center GmbH
Europaplatz 3
69115 Heidelberg, Germany

www.ingramcontent.com/pod-product-compliance
Lightning Source LLC
LaVergne TN
LVHW011826060526
838200LV00053B/3916